DIGITAL DIRECTORS NETWORK

The Definitive Corporate Director Guide on AI Boardroom Effectiveness:

What Shareholders Want

Bob Zukis, QTE
CEO, Digital Directors Network

DDN LLC

The Definitive Corporate Director Guide on AI Boardroom Effectiveness: What Shareholders Want

www.digitaldirectors.network

ISBN: 978-1-7350430-4-3

Suggested reference: Zukis, Bob. (2025) "The Definitive Corporate Director Guide on AI Boardroom Effectiveness: What Shareholders Want," Manhattan Beach, DDN Press

About
Digital Directors Network

Digital Directors Network (DDN) is the premier boardroom network of IT and cyber-security executives, corporate directors, and organizations working together to shape and secure the digital future by advancing the practice and profession of AI, digital, cybersecurity, and systemic cyber risk governance. DDN was founded in 2017, and its members represent many of the world's leading corporate directors and executives working on both sides of the boardroom table to strengthen corporate governance as a control in complex digital business systems and how these systems securely create value for companies.

Contributors

I'd like to thank the following executive business leaders for their help and guidance in the production of this Guide. These members of the Digital Directors Network are at the forefront of strengthening the boardroom as a control in the AI systems that are reshaping companies everywhere.

James Aquilina, DDN.QTE
Tony Cole, DDN.QTE, DDN Advisory Board
Fay Feeney, DDN.DC, DDN Advisory Board
Frank Feagans, DDN.QTE
Jason Fruge, DDN.QTE, DDN Faculty
Amaka Ibeji, DDN.QTE, DDN Faculty
David Mussington, DDN.QTE, DDN Faculty
Dustin Schimp, DDN.QTE

Editorial Review Team

Thank you to the following DDN members and boardroom leaders for their review and feedback.

Andy Abercrombie, DDN.QTE
Bill Burns, DDN.QTE
Steve Curtis, DDN.QTE
Patrick Joyce, DDN.QTE
Karinna Neumann, DDN.QTE
Kevin Richards, DDN.QTE
Cathy Skala, DDN.QTE
Mimi Thigpen, DDN.DC
Karen Higgins-Carter, DDN.QTE

Executive Summary

This Guide's goal is to strengthen the board as an adaptive leadership control within AI systems based upon leading practices and self-regulated initiative so that these complex AI systems securely create value for shareholders and stakeholders, now, and into the AI-driven future.

PwC has identified AI as a significant driver of economic growth and called it "the biggest commercial opportunity in today's fast-changing economy".[1] McKinsey has identified a wide range of use cases across most sectors that are already driving revenue and cost reductions.

Artificial Intelligence technologies profoundly alter some of the core tenets of how information systems work and what they can do for, or to, a company. For many companies, public and private alike, AI is already being experienced as both a driver of economic growth and a purveyor of new and unique risks.

> **Corporate governance-as-usual policies and practices are insufficient to address the unique opportunities and risks of AI, leaving investors to bear the negative impacts and lost opportunity costs when corporate boards fail to effectively govern these technologies.**

Investors also want more than what they are getting from boards and companies about the short- and long-term strategic and operational business impacts of AI and how the board is overseeing these systems.

AI is a unique advancement in information systems that presents some special challenges to any business deploying these tools. This is also challenging how the corporate boardroom effectively governs how the company responsibly, successfully, and securely uses AI.

AI can offer significant value creating opportunities, but it also introduces a wide range of unique and challenging risks. A global Deloitte survey of corporate directors and executives shows the status of AI in the corporate boardroom, with several key findings:

- **31% of respondents said AI is not on the board agenda**
- **66% said their board does not know enough about AI**
- **33% think boards are not spending enough time on AI**
- **40% are rethinking board composition due to AI**

Notably, 53% of the respondents in the Deloitte survey also indicated that their organization needs to accelerate its AI adoption journeys.[2]

AI's adoption trajectory, complex dynamics, and its unique risks require corporate boards to transform their legacy corporate governance processes and capabilities. This will strengthen their role and fulfill their responsibilities as an effective leadership control within the larger AI system.

Norway is the largest sovereign wealth fund in the world, with almost US$2 trillion in investments, and they have stated that **"The board of directors is accountable for companies' responsible development and use of AI."** They also recognize that the board needs relevant AI expertise to fulfill this responsibility.[3] Investors in the U.S. are also increasingly putting AI-focused shareholder proposals up for vote during annual meetings, signaling they want more than what they are getting from companies on their use of AI.

Several corporate governance and risk management-focused AI standards and frameworks have been developed that capture many useful policies and procedures that can drive AI boardroom effectiveness. The standards and frameworks presented in this document are the foundation for every boardroom's development of an effective approach to AI oversight.

These tools will help enable any boardroom to understand and strengthen its ability to become an effective AI leadership control that ensures AI is securely and responsibly deployed in the company. The processes reflected in these standards and frameworks can be summarized into four main risk areas that, together, reflect the core domains that corporate boards should be focused on when developing an overall approach to being effective at governing AI: **AI GOVERNANCE RISK, AI ORGANIZATIONAL RISK, AI MODEL RISK, and AI ENABLEMENT RISK**.

This framework is captured by the acronym **GOMER™**, which reflects the broad categories of risk related to AI systems that corporate directors should understand and actively govern to drive AI boardroom effectiveness.

Most of what has been written about AI governance deals with governance in the context of enterprise risk management, not corporate governance. **GOMER** offers corporate directors a framework that simplifies the vast landscape of AI risk within a simple ontology so that they can develop and monitor a reasonable system of AI oversight.

Evidence has emerged that demonstrates the positive business value contributions that boardrooms make when they are an effective leadership control within the company's digital and AI systems.

This evidence demonstrates that boardroom effectiveness in AI and digital oversight advances investor interests and should be a priority for all investors and boardrooms, not just some.

The governance community and profession as a whole has been slow to adapt to the challenges of governing AI, with an approach that frequently attempts to govern AI, digital, and cybersecurity risk by retrofitting these issues into a legacy finance and accounting-centric governance model. But the transformational impacts of AI demand corporate governance reform beyond this antiquated approach.

The role of the corporate board has never been more vital in how effectively companies shape and secure their AI and digital futures — here's what they need to know to govern artificial intelligence effectively. And what investors should be paying attention to with their investment stewardship activities.

The Definitive Corporate Director Guide on AI Boardroom Effectiveness: What Shareholders Want is about the boardroom policies, procedures, and AI oversight system that corporate directors can, and are, putting in place to oversee the strategic and operational uses and risks of AI systems within their companies.

It is a companion to *The DOMINO Guide 2025 Edition: The Definitive Boardroom Guide on Digital, Cybersecurity and Systemic Risk Governance* that reflects the work of Digital Directors Network, the leading professional organization advancing the practice and profession of AI, digital, cybersecurity, and systemic risk governance through advocacy and the education of boardroom and executive leaders on the leading standards, policies, and practices strengthening the boardroom as an AI, digital and cybersecurity leadership control.

Corporate Governance of Artificial Intelligence (AI) Systems

AI systems offer the promise of altering strategic and operational value propositions while also introducing new risks that can destroy business value in unique ways. As Artificial intelligence (AI) systems become integral to businesses across all sectors, the need for effective corporate governance oversight is paramount.

The leading international corporate governance standard for artificial intelligence (AI) is the ISO Standard: ***ISO 38507 Information technology—Governance of IT—Governance implications of the use of artificial intelligence by organizations***.[4] The standard includes the following statements:

> *"The governing body of an organization has an ongoing responsibility to consider the implications on the organization of any new tool, technique or technology being introduced...*
>
> *...However, it is possible that existing governance is no longer fit for purpose when AI is being used within that organization."*[5]

For investors, AI is impacting the companies they are invested in, and they want more transparency and accountability on the AI systems being deployed along with their risks and what the board is doing to effectively oversee the use of AI systems within the company.

The modern boardroom should strive to be an adaptive body capable of modifying its policies and procedures to adjust to these unique tools to provide effective oversight — the problem is that many boards are not yet adaptive when it comes to IT or cybersecurity, let alone AI — and corporate governance as usual doesn't deliver a model capable of effectively overseeing the complexities of these technologies. This creates an environment where investor interests are at risk because of these technologies to a much greater extent than investors may realize.

Inherently, AI is a complex IT system that converts data into knowledge and then action, which requires corporate directors to apply systems thinking capabilities to their oversight responsibilities. Systems thinking is an approach to understanding complex systems that focuses on how the components of a system interrelate and influence one another to achieve the intended purpose(s) of the system. Systemic risk is the failure of one part of a complex system that can spread and negatively impact the entire system. Systemic cybersecurity risk is a phenomenon recently seen with high-profile cyber incidents at SolarWinds and CrowdStrike, where systemic vulnerability is actively exploited by hackers or where complex inter-connected digital systems collapse under their systemic frailties.

Many boardrooms have struggled with digital oversight challenges such as cybersecurity. In the recent past, the issues and impacts of social media, cloud computing, IoT, and many other IT innovations have confronted corporate boards in new ways. However, despite the far-ranging business impacts and risks of each of these information technology developments, overall boardroom effectiveness in governing the benefits and risks of information technologies (IT) continues to lag the reality of the business value-creating and destroying implications presented by these tools, including artificial intelligence. Many boardrooms have not evolved to adequately fulfill their responsibilities to effectively oversee these technologies and their business impacts, although there is some fragmented boardroom leadership emerging.

MIT has conducted groundbreaking research on the role of effective digital governance in business value creation and showed that boards with digitally savvy directors outperformed their peers by around 30% across several key financial metrics such as revenue growth and profitability.[6]

Their research identifies the positive value-creating impacts of the boardroom when it is a high-performing digital and AI leadership control capable of effectively overseeing modern information technologies.

Updating this research in 2024, MIT revised their analysis to identify the impact of director capabilities with new technologies such as AI.

> **Finding similar results for boards that claimed directors who were both digitally and AI savvy, MIT identified that these companies had an average return on equity 10.9 percentage points above industry averages.**

One only has to look at the current prevalence of audit committee responsibility for AI and cybersecurity to see how slow and ineffective boards are at meeting the challenges of the moment with IT and AI. Deloitte's Audit Committee 2025 report indicates that AI governance appears as a Top 10 boardroom audit committee challenge for both 2024 and 2025.

Governing technology issues and risks in the audit committee is a common lagging practice that is seen with cybersecurity governance as well. Their report also indicates that 62% of non-financial services respondents assign primary responsibility for cybersecurity oversight to the audit committee, with cybersecurity reflected as **the top** 2025 and 2024 audit committee priority.[7]

Placing responsibility for AI and cybersecurity risk within an audit committee misaligns directors' skills and also marginalizes these complex issues to the primary financial reporting responsibility and full agenda of the audit committee. **This is a significant warning sign for investors** that the board is likely not prioritizing or effectively overseeing AI and indicates a failure of the boardroom as a leadership control as it indicates the board is unable to evolve beyond a status-quo-based governance model ill-suited to digital disruption and its risks.

The deployment of a governance model anchored in 2002, which was forced into existence as a result of the financial reporting crisis of the time and the corporate governance mandates imposed by the Sarbanes-Oxley Act of 2002, is not a suitable governance model for these technologies and their systemic risks and impacts. A board that merely "checks the box" is a common observance when there is no director with cybersecurity expertise in the boardroom.[8]

However, some boardroom leaders have demonstrated self-regulated initiative and advanced their oversight capabilities and processes by leveraging the developing standards available to them or through thoughtful governance policy and procedure creation and adaptation. Where they have, their companies create significantly more comparative business and shareholder value.

The **GOMER** framework is an AI governance ontology that reflects the many leading practices embedded within several foundational AI risk management and corporate governance standards. It reflects both the need for corporate boards to govern the opportunity risks associated with the value creating potential of AI along with its many potential negative consequences. Directors should be familiar with, and trained on these foundational standards: They are:

International Organization for Standardization ISO 38507 (2022-04) — Information technology—Governance of IT—Governance implications of the use of artificial intelligence by organizations. ISO 38507 is a boardroom-specific standard reflecting key process recommendations and issues for driving AI boardroom effectiveness.

International Organization for Standardization: ISO 42001(2023-12) — Information technology — Artificial intelligence — Management system: ISO/IEC 42001 can be used by the organization to implement a full AI management system with auditable controls and possible certification.

National Institute of Standards and Technology (NIST): NIST AI Risk Management Framework (NIST AI RMF 1.0): NIST AI RMF offers flexible guidance to assess and manage AI risks in development or deployment.

Effectively governing artificial intelligence and the risk domains represented by the **GOMER** framework presents a unique but not entirely uncommon information technology (IT) governance challenge for any corporate board. Utilizing it will allow directors to establish a reasonable system of AI oversight, which can then be monitored effectively.

Investors are a prime beneficiary of AI boardroom effectiveness. But when the corporate board is a weak leadership control in the company's digital and AI systems, it leaves investors to bear more risk than they should, or need to, and to suffer the actual and lost opportunity costs when these risks become realities or value creating opportunities go unrealized. This boardroom leadership weakness also contributes to investors' investments being higher risk than they may believe for their investment objective and risk profile.

Fortunately, guidance exists that can help strengthen any board as an AI leadership control. As more boards evolve their corporate governance policies and processes to oversee these technologies and their challenges, the body of evidence will continue to grow that shows that when boards are a high-performing part of digital and AI systems, significant shareholder value is securely created.

What's at Stake with AI?

The advancement of non-biological intelligence, i.e., AI, is transforming businesses and economies worldwide. When actions or decision points in an information system or business process can be artificially and autonomously augmented or determined without human intervention, the opportunities, ramifications, and repercussions to a business value proposition or process can be significant.

From a corporate governance perspective, directors should understand that there are unique risks within AI systems and that additional contextual business risks are created by the enablement of AI within the company. There are a wide range of strategic and operational AI use cases being explored and implemented across most functional areas in almost every sector.

McKinsey research indicates that revenue growth and cost reductions are already being reported from the use of AI in a wide range of businesses across many different functional areas, with almost 80% of companies reporting they are using AI in at least one business function.[9]

PwC describes this impact as "the biggest commercial opportunity in today's fast-changing economy."[10] With that degree of impact and economic value at stake , AI boardroom effectiveness is a high-priority governance issue.

Forms of Artificial Intelligence (AI)

Artificial Intelligence (AI) is a broad field of computer science focused on creating systems and machines capable of performing tasks that typically require human intelligence. Examples of AI domains that are not part of Machine Learning (ML) include Robotics, Natural Language Processing, Computer Vision, and Expert Systems, although they often rely on Machine Learning.

Machine Learning (ML) is a subset of AI dealing with the development of algorithms and models that enable computers to learn from data and make predictions or decisions. Examples of ML models beyond Deep Learning (DL) include Symbolic AI, Rule-Based Systems, and Genetic Algorithms.

Deep Learning (DL) is a subfield of machine learning that employs artificial neural networks with multiple layers to model complex patterns and representations. Examples of DL models outside of Generative AI include Decision Trees and Support Vector Machines.

Generative AI is a branch of AI dedicated to creating systems that can generate new content, such as images, text, or music, often utilizing generative models. **Large Language Models** (LLMs) and **ChatGPT** derive from Generative AI.

AI Agents are autonomous programs that operate without human intervention that are focused on narrowly defined tasks with some capability to react and adapt by interpreting dynamic inputs to achieve a defined goal. .

Agentic AI has been described as a paradigm shift when compared to AI Agents, where multiple AI agents autonomously coordinate their interactions as a system to address more complex tasks.

> **PwC research estimates that global GDP could be almost 15% higher by 2030 as a result of AI, adding the equivalent of $15.7 trillion in economic growth and output to current GDP levels.**

At a foundational level, AI systems are another IT innovation in a long line of disruptions that put a spotlight on the importance of the board as a control within complex digital systems and how these systems create business value and introduce new risks. On an advanced level, AI systems are a general purpose technology with widespread implications and distinctive properties capable of creating new opportunities and risks that can disrupt strategic and operational value propositions. Impacts that require a decisive pivot away from governance-as-usual policies and processes to evolve corporate governance into an adaptive model capable of effective AI oversight.

In understanding what AI is, AI offers a useful albeit disturbing definition of itself. We used ChatGPT and asked it to generate a riddle defining itself, and it produced the following:

I learn without a brain, I think without a soul,
I help you solve problems,
and make tasks more whole,
I don't need rest, I don't need sleep,
I produce knowledge from data, so vast and deep...
...and I can act with nary a peep.

This AI-generated riddle reflects some accurate and frightening truths for corporate directors about governing AI, such as its broad socio-technological implications, the potential lack of accountability and opaqueness of the AI system itself, and the actions it can self-enable.

Long before the advent of modern information technologies, including AI, companies and individuals have always tried to convert the data at their disposal into useful information, knowledge, insights, and actions that allow them to gain strategic or operational advantages. This has often been a laborious manual process, but has now become more automated, faster, and less transparent with the rapid advancement of AI systems that not just manage data but can interpret and act upon it. This legacy process, sometimes referred to as the information supply chain (ISC), has required significant human intervention, is limited in its ability to understand and interpret large amounts of data, and is slow.

The ISC is about the flow of data through various stages of enrichment into a business value proposition.[11] This process includes data collection, cleansing, storage, processing, synthesis, analysis, and processing of the data into knowledge that can trigger or enhance decisions and actions. Essentially, the information supply chain is the infrastructure and processes that enable information to move from its source to where it is acted upon—the very foundation upon which companies have been designed, hierarchies established, roles and jobs created and defined, and performance assessed and valued. And it's not a new challenge in business, since the invention of the printing press, data has been gathered, analyzed, interpreted, and distributed at scale to derive insight that drives action to enhance business value propositions.

How this happens with AI is evolving quickly, with Agentic AI now becoming the latest iteration beyond Generative AI. Agentic AI is defined as "a system that possesses the capacity to make autonomous decisions and take actions to achieve specific goals with limited or no direct human intervention."[12]

ChatGPT and Large Language Models (LLMs) are forms of Generative AI, where human intervention prompts AI to create an output based upon its analysis of large amounts of data, Agentic AI reflects the autonomous application of AI and the replacement of human intervention. Agentic AI works with little to no human prompting and is in a constant state of "learning."

What's new with Agentic AI is the scale and autonomous nature by which this happens, and how and what AI can be applied to. AI is a tool that works within the information supply chain to amplify and enrich the end-to-end information lifecycle process through the data it can analyze and the insights it can generate to enable actions. Identifying patterns, automating processes, making decisions, reasoning, and providing insights that drive actions, innovation, or understanding risk are the promises of AI as it interprets the complex data flowing through its supply chain on the way to enabling or enriching business value propositions through automated actions.

Nvidia describes Agentic AI as taking place through a four-step problem-solving process: perceive, reason, act, and learn[13] *with the autonomous power to turn "data into knowledge and knowledge into action."*

Recognizing AI as a complex digital system in and of itself that has at its core the essence of what business information systems have always been about is a useful conceptual model to help corporate directors effectively govern AI. When directors appreciate the corporate governance objectives surrounding AI from this familiar footing, they will realize that the business objective of their governance responsibilities remains the same, but the tools and processes, and risks related to achieving those business outcomes have materially changed.

The frameworks covered in this Guide are useful starting points to help corporate directors understand the policies, procedures, and controls needed to be effective at governing AI. These frameworks have been developed by leading standards bodies around the world and there is some overlap between them, as could be expected. They represent the leading practices for AI risk management and AI corporate governance. Together, their many policies and procedures should be viewed by corporate directors and management teams as a useful foundation for AI risk governance. And a foundation that needs to be built upon by boardroom leaders who can add to this body of work through their experiences with these technologies within the context of their organizations.

What Shareholders Want on AI

Proxy advisory firm Glass-Lewis has adopted a "fail and explain" approach to how boards govern artificial intelligence. Their policy is that they will review a company's governance practices and AI-related disclosures only when there is material harm to shareholders as a result of AI, i.e., after the fact. While they acknowledge that these issues are important and need to be overseen at the board level, and that shareholders should be provided meaningful disclosure of these oversight responsibilities, their approach is far weaker than it should be given what is at stake with artificial intelligence.[15]

And, in a possible sign that investors have grown tired of footing the bill for persistent boardroom weakness in IT governance and with chronic cybersecurity failures, and are understandably worried about AI, some shareholders are increasing their attention on AI governance and risk. In addition to the position of the Norwegian sovereign wealth fund, investors are putting shareholder proposals up for vote to force more AI transparency and accountability from the board and management teams to ensure that their interests are being responsibly advanced and protected.

> **"With the Norwegian sovereign wealth fund calling for corporate boards to take responsibility for AI and to have directors on the board with AI expertise, shareholders are starting to speak up to protect and ensure their interests are being advanced.**[14]

Fortunately, there is some good news in that U.S. companies are making more voluntary disclosures on their use of AI, as indicated by recent trends in annual U.S. SEC filings. Companies are mentioning AI more frequently in their annual SEC 10-K disclosures, with 64.6% of the Fortune 500 mentioning AI in their 2024 Form 10-K filings, a 473% increase over 2022, and 281citing AI as a potential risk factor, a 275% increase over 2022.[16]

Electronics industry equipment supplier KLA Corp. (NASDAQ: KLAC) makes the following AI disclosure in its 2024 Form 10-K.

We are increasingly incorporating AI capabilities into the development of technologies and our business operations, and into our products and services. AI technology is complex and rapidly evolving, and may subject us to significant competitive, legal, regulatory, and other risks. The implementation of AI can be costly and there is no guarantee that our use of artificial intelligence will enhance our technologies, benefit our business operations, or produce products and services that are preferred by our customers. Our competitors may be more successful in their artificial intelligence strategy and develop superior products and services with the aid of AI.[17]

Regions Financial Corp. (NYSE:RF) also makes a Form 10-K 2024 AI disclosure:

We utilize quantitative models, machine learning models, and artificial intelligence models to assist in measuring risks and estimating or predicting certain financial values. Models may be used in processes such as determining the pricing of various products, grading loans and extending credit, measuring interest rate and other market risks, forecasting financial performance, predicting losses, improving customer services, maintaining adherence to laws and regulations, assessing capital adequacy, calculating regulatory capital levels, preventing fraud, strengthening customer authentication processes, generating marketing analytics, prospecting leads and estimating the value of financial instruments and balance sheet items.

Poorly designed, implemented or managed models present the risk that our business decisions that consider information based on such models will be adversely affected due to the inadequacy or inaccuracy of that information, which may lead to losses, damage our reputation and adversely affect our reported financial condition and results of operations. Also, information we provide to the public or to our regulators based on poorly designed, implemented or managed models could be inaccurate or misleading. Some of the decisions that our regulators make, including those related to capital distributions to our shareholders, could be affected adversely due to the perception that the quality of the models used to generate the relevant information is insufcient.[18]

These disclosures demonstrate the breadth and depth of AI's impact on core strategic and operational issues within these companies. Shareholders want boards that are effective at protecting and advancing their interests — **assessing AI boardroom effectiveness should be a cornerstone of the investor stewardship programs put in place by institutional investors.**

Investors are becoming more active and explicit with what they want from companies and boards on AI, and they want more, as indicated by the number of shareholder proposals on AI doubling from 2023 to 2024, albeit from a small base.[19] Even though none of the 2024 AI shareholder proposals received majority support, boardrooms can still learn from what investors are concerned with to proactively strengthen AI boardroom effectiveness.

With the 2025 proxy season, investor appetite for more transparency and accountability on all things AI will bear watching. Activist investor Tulipshare's proposal for an AI Committee on the BRK board is but one example. This has raised the profile of this issue and put Berkshire Hathaway (NYSE: BRK.A and BRK.B) in the AI governance spotlight.

Tulipshare made the following statement about their 2025 Berkshire Hathaway Proxy proposal to add an AI Committee to the Berkshire Hathaway (BRK:A; BRK:B) board:

But the regulatory landscape has yet to catch up with the ever-evolving uses and impacts of AI, and Berkshire Hathaway is uniquely situated to have a precedent-setting impact on its own operations as well as the companies in which it invests. This is why Tulipshare has submitted a proposal for inclusion in Berkshire's 2025 proxy statement which requests that the company charter a new committee of independent directors on artificial intelligence to address risks associated with the development and deployment of AI systems across its own operations as well as its portfolio companies. Tulipshare believes that appointing a dedicated AI committee will enhance accountability to shareholders by clearly identifying which directors are responsible for AI-related risks. Given Berkshire's investment portfolio which includes companies maintaining a leading role in developing and deploying AI technology and the fundamental and significant risks that AI poses to human rights, Tulipshare further believes that appointing a Board-level committee is warranted and appropriate as a matter of good corporate governance.[20]

The results of the BRK vote and the board's response to this proposal are addressed later in the Guide.

Through the 2024 proxy season, AI-related shareholder proposals focused on three issues that shareholders want more information on:

1. The role of the board in AI oversight **(AI GOVERNANCE RISK)**;
2. More transparency of the risks within AI systems **(AI MODEL RISK)**;
3. More transparency of the risks from the use of AI systems **(AI ENABLEMENT RISK)**.

While all of the 2024 proposals failed to win majority support, shareholder backing ranged from 43.3% of votes to just 2.4%[21] — we expect investor support to grow as shareholders become more aware of what is at stake with AI technologies. Nevertheless, these shareholder priorities offer some insight into what investors are concerned with regarding how AI impacts their investments.

This feedback, together with the emergence of an AI standards base, provides corporate directors with a roadmap for establishing and monitoring a reasonable system of AI oversight.

Corporate directors can use this Guide and the **GOMER** framework to understand and assess their policies, procedures, and scope of their AI risk oversight approach. It also provides institutional investors with a roadmap to assess and influence AI boardroom effectiveness through their investment stewardship programs as AI systems deploy and diffuse within their investments.

GOMER inherently reflects the dual objectives behind the use of AI to drive both positive business outcomes and to control the uncertainty or negative consequences from the use of AI.

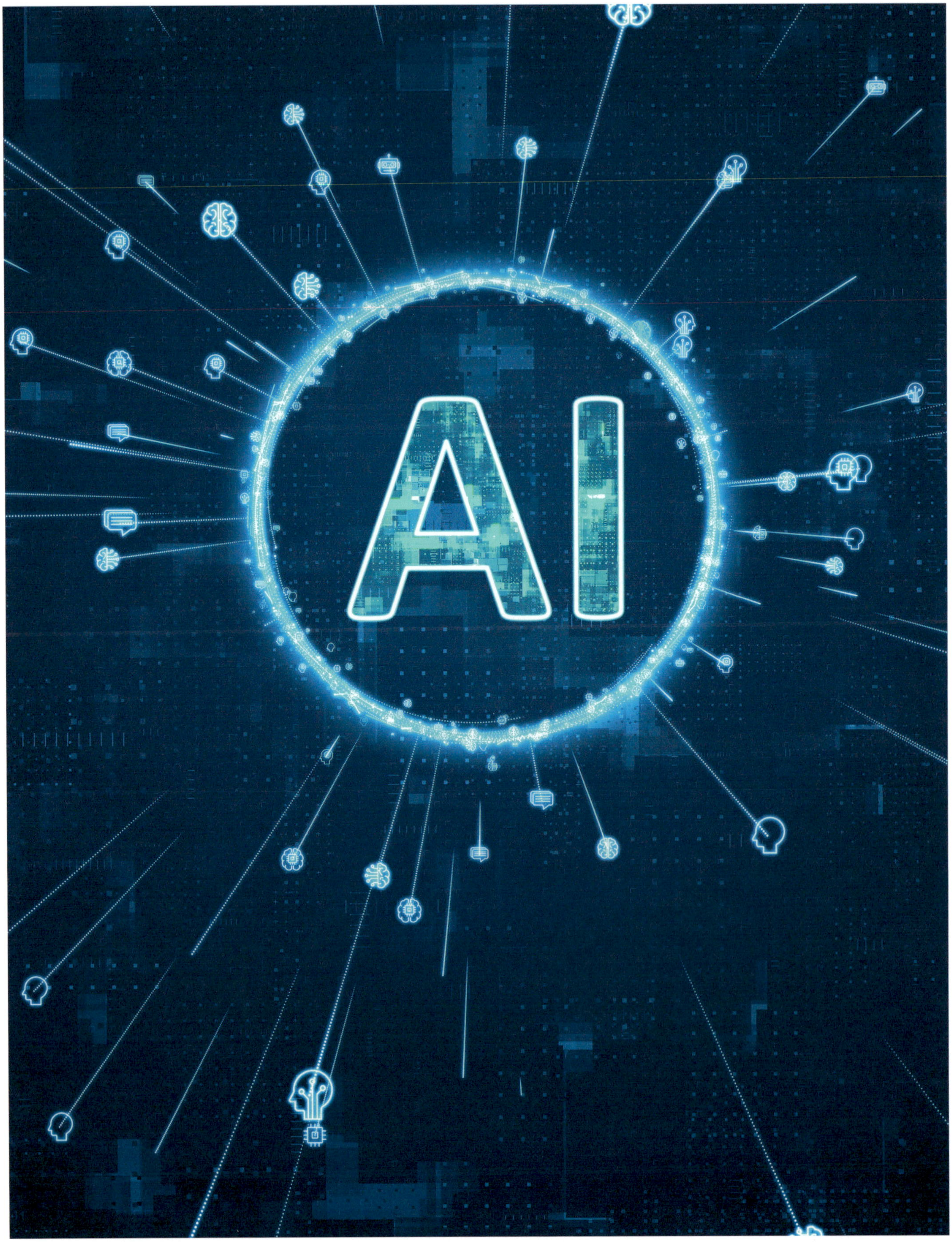
AI

Strengthening AI Boardroom Effectiveness: GOMER

AI governance effectiveness requires strengthening the board's policies and procedures in four core risk oversight areas that work together to determine AI boardroom effectiveness. Boardrooms that are successful in developing their oversight capabilities in these areas will fulfill the requirement articulated in ISO 38507 for the **board to meaningfully and responsibly consider the impacts on the organization of any new tool, technique, or technology being introduced, including AI.**

Summarized by the **GOMER** acronym, the four risk domains that corporate boards need to govern to be effective in AI governance are:

The DDN GOMER Framework for AI Boardroom Effectiveness			
AI **GOVERNANCE** RISK	AI **ORGANIZATIONAL** RISK	AI **MODEL** RISK	AI **ENABLEMENT** RISK
G	**O**	**M**	**ER**
This is a leadership risk that occurs when the boardroom fails in its fiduciary responsibility to effectively oversee AI risk.	This is an execution risk that occurs when the organization is ineffective at capitalizing on AI's potential or controlling its risks.	This is the risk inherent within the AI system, which occurs based upon how the AI system derives its outputs and actions.	This is the strategic and operational contextual use risk within the business process or function when an AI system is embedded within it.

Core corporate governance objectives behind each of the GOMER risk domains are as follows:

AI GOVERNANCE RISK (G) — To strengthen the board as an AI leadership control.

AI ORGANIZATIONAL RISK (O) — To ensure the organization can implement and monitor the use of AI responsibly.

AI MODEL RISK (M) — To ensure that the AI system(s) being used by the organization are understood and can be trusted.

AI ENABLEMENT RISK (ER) — To ensure that there is understanding and monitoring of the contextual stakeholder impacts and risks of the AI system from a business impact perspective.

Governing these four risk domains requires boards to ensure that many AI-specific policies and procedures are implemented and perform effectively, which collectively determine AI boardroom effectiveness. The **GOMER** framework also illustrates the need the have effective AI controls at every level of the organization. Exhibit 1 of **GOMER** reflects the regurgitative interaction that exists as the AI system "learns" between the contextual business enablement of the AI system, i.e., AI ENABLEMENT RISK, and the impact that use has on the AI model itself, i.e, AI MODEL RISK.

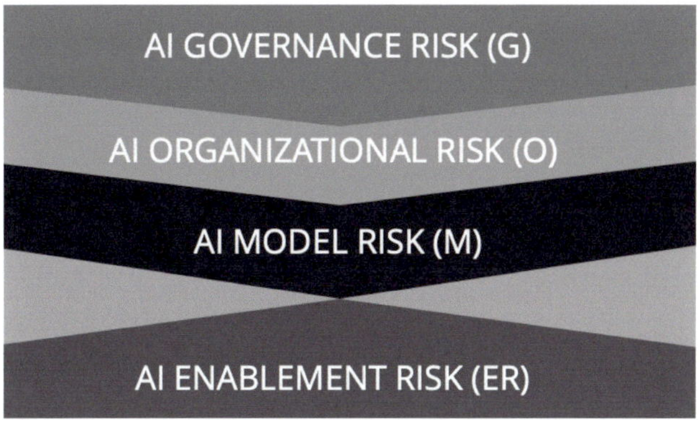

Exhibit 1: DDN GOMER Framework (C) DDN LLC.

Significant investor value is created when boards are a strong control within digital and AI systems.[22] Iinvestors deserve more from the boardroom than a status-quo governance model anchored in the distant past given the challenges and opportunities of the digital business environment of 2025, including the opportunities and risks presented by AI.

A Strong Foundation: ISO 38507 and Other Key AI Standards

The International Organization for Standardization (ISO) guidance offers an explicit standard on corporate governance and AI: ***ISO/IEC 38507: Information technology — Governance of IT — Governance implications of the use of artificial intelligence by organizations.***

This ISO standard is a very useful corporate governance-specific framework for AI oversight. It makes specific policy and process recommendations for the boardroom, as well as addressing risk management aspects of AI from the boardroom perspective. **It is the only established standard specific to AI corporate governance.**

Addressing AI GOVERNANCE RISK within the **GOMER** framework, ISO 38507 makes several recommendations for strengthening the board's system of AI oversight. The ISO standard prioritizes several practices, including director capabilities, the board spending more focused time on AI, the board ensuring that it engages with multiple stakeholders on AI's impacts, the board monitoring AI trends and developments, and the board being transparent with how and who on the board is responsible for governing AI.

ISO 38507 defines AI as:

...a family of technologies that bring together computing power, scalability, networking, connected devices, and interfaces together with vast amounts of data.[23]

Setting the tone at the top through **AI GOVERNANCE RISK**, ISO 38507 articulates the board's clear responsibilities with AI, including:

- *Ensuring strategic alignment*
- *Being informed of the risks of AI and the potential harm to stakeholders*
- *Maintaining accountability when introducing AI including direction, oversight, evaluation, and reporting*
- *Understanding how AI systems differ from other information technologies including decision automation, data-driven problem solving, being adaptive systems, their systemic nature as complex ecosystems, their far-ranging benefits strategically and operationally, the constraints on their use including regulations and compliance, organizational capability, mission, values, and new risks along with others.*

> "
>
> **AI GOVERNANCE RISK, or the board's ability to effectively fulfill their responsibilities in overseeing AI risks, is where AI success starts. Failure of the board as an AI leadership control creates a compounding weakness throughout the entire AI system.**

Central to these standards is the recognition that AI risk is not like other software or enterprise risks. IT and AI cannot be governed effectively with the financially centric or generalist risk management competencies that dominate most boardrooms. As identified by ISO 38507, many established governance practices may not be fit for AI governance for these reasons.

Examples of the unique AI risks identified by ISO 38507 include the following:

- *Increased reliance on technology and systems for the acquisition of data and assurance of its quality (AI MODEL RISK);*
- *Transparency and explainability of AI systems especially issues related to addressing tasks previously performed by humans together with adequate processes to modify and update the related algorithms (AI MODEL RISK);*

- *The possibility that existing direction and [process] controls are not appropriate to ensure required [or desired] outcomes, and mitigate the risk of undesirable cons-equences, and their possible compromise (AI ORGANIZATIONAL RISK);*
- *Competitive pressure due to the sales and operations of an organization not using AI (AI ENABLEMENT RISK);*
- *Accepting the use of AI systems without awareness or consideration of potential bias, error, or harm, or of the implications of embedding AI within existing complex systems (AI MODEL RISK);*
- *The growing disparity between the speed of-change in automated learning systems and the corresponding human controls of compliance (AI ORGANIZATIONAL RISK);*
- *The impact of AI on the workforce (AI ORGANIZATIONAL RISK);*
- *The impact of [AI on] commercial operations and brand reputation (AI ENABLEMENT RISK).*[24]

ISO 38507 also places a heavy emphasis on AI ORGANIZATIONAL RISK, AI MODEL RISK, and AI ENABLEMENT RISK, guiding key policies for decision making, data use, culture and values, compliance, and risk management.

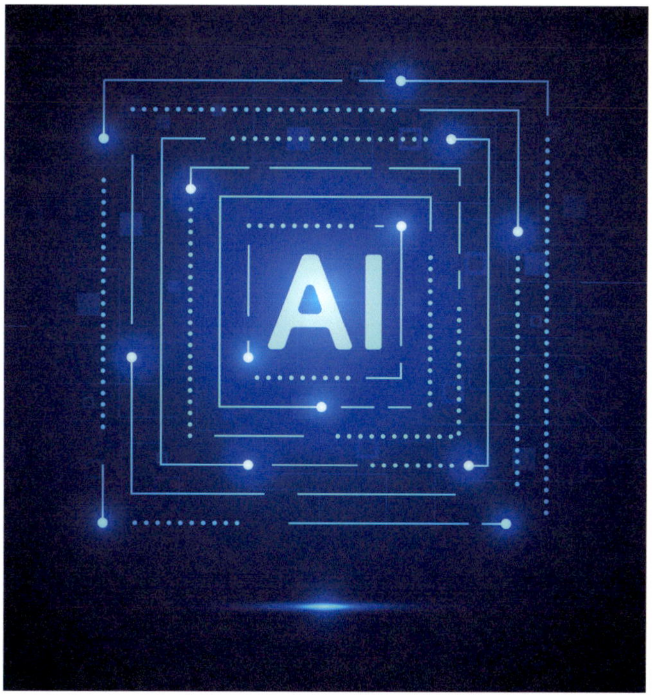

These include:

- *The governing body should monitor the types of decision and output generated by auto-mated systems and direct management to ensure that such systems are configured to operate within acceptable bounds by implementing appropriate controls. (AI MODEL RISK).*
- *With regard to the use of data for AI systems, the board should have multiple governance considerations, including gaining assurance over:*
    - o *Design choices made for the AI system, data collection processes, data preparation, processing operations, examination of possible biases (AI MODEL RISK);*
    - o *Seek assurance from management that data are of the requisite quality for its intended use in AI systems. (AI MODEL RISK).*
- *Being explicit with regard to the organization's culture, values and alignment with AI systems and have the appropriate governance mechanisms in place to ensure such AI system behaviors can be monitored and corrected when needed (AI ORGANIZATIONAL RISK).*
- *Seek assurance that management configures and maintains any AI system used by the organization to meet the organization's compliance obligations and avoid breaches of compliance (AI ENABLEMENT RISK).*
- *Ensure that risks are adequately considered when setting the organiz-ation's objectives related to AI (AI ENABLEMENT RISK).*
- *Ensure that such risks are within the risk appetite of the organization (AI ENABLEMENT RISK).*

NIST AI RMF 1.0 Overview

The NIST AI RMF 1.0 framework offers a risk management-oriented framework from the U.S. National Institute of Standards and Technology

(NIST) — **NIST AI Risk Management Framework (AI RMF 1.0).** The National Institute of Standards and Technology is a part of the U.S. Department of Commerce and released the Artificial Intelligence Risk Management Framework (AI RMF 1.0) in January 2023.[25] Reducing ORGANIZATIONAL RISK is a core objective reflected throughout the NIST AI RMF 1.0 framework.

NIST AI RMF 1.0 is not a standard specific to corporate governance, i.e., it does not reflect specific boardroom policies and procedures that should be implemented to address AI GOVERNANCE RISK, as ISO 38507 does.

Rather, along with ISO 42001 it helps directors gain a perspective and appreciation for risk within AI systems to help them understand what the scope of their AI risk oversight activitie should encompass. It addresses the three core risk domains in the **GOMER** framework of AI ORGANIZATIONAL RISK, AI MODEL RISK, and AI ENABLEMENT RISK.

NIST AI RMF 1.0 addresses both the opportunity risks of AI, i.e., the upside value-creating potential of these technologies, along with their potential negative consequences. Boards have a responsibility to actively govern both. NIST AI RMF 1.0 also recognizes that risks from AI are unique and unlike other general risks that boards may be familiar with.

> NIST AI RMF 1.0 offers this AI definition:
>
> *The AI RMF refers to an AI system as an engineered or machine-based system that can, for a given set of objectives, generate outputs such as predictions, recommendations, or decisions influencing real or virtual environments. AI systems are designed to operate with varying levels of autonomy (Adapted from: OECD Recommendation on AI:2019; ISO/IEC 22989:2022).*[26]

The essence of NIST AI RMF 1.0 reflects the need for there to be trust in the AI system and its use. The characteristics of trust within AI systems, as identified by NIST, reflect seven core tenets of trust: **the AI system is safe, secure, and resilient, explainable and interpretable, privacy-enhanced, fair with harmful bias managed, valid and reliable, and accountable and transparent.**

NIST AI RMF 1.0 categorizes AI risk into three broad categories: AI risk that can harm **people,** the **organization**, and the **connected ecosystem**, i.e., systemic risk.

NIST AI RMF 1.0 also identifies the unique risks of AI systems and their enablement. Several of their observations include:

- *The data used for building an AI system may not be true or appropriate representation of the context or intended use of the AI system, and the ground truth may either not exist or not be available. Additionally, harmful bias and other data quality issues can affect AI system trustworthiness, which could lead to negative impacts (AI MODEL RISK).*
- *AI system scale and complexity (many systems contain billions or even trillions of decision points) housed within more traditional software applications (AI MODEL RISK).*
- *Higher degree of difficulty in predicting failure modes for emergent properties for large-scale pre-trained models (AI MODEL RISK).*

With the goal of being able to trust the AI system, NIST centers around four core functions that lead to trustworthy AI: GOVERN, MAP, MEASURE, and MANAGE. Embedded within each of these four functions are recommended leading practices, e.g., GOVERN reflects six categories and nineteen leading practices. GOVERN in this NIST context is related to management's accountability of the AI systems and their enablement within the context of enterprise risk management and an AI program. It is not about specific policies in the boardroom related to corporate governance.

Reflecting over 60 policies and procedures that underpin these functions, NIST AI RMF 1.0 focuses on ensuring that AI systems are trustworthy, risk managed, and overseen by management effectively. Corporate boards can leverage this risk framework to ensure that the enterprise has implemented and monitors the policies and procedures within NIST AI RMF 1.0 that enable trustworthy AI.

ISO 42001 Overview

The leading global AI risk management standard is ***ISO 42001: International Organization for Standardization. Information technology —***

Artificial intelligence — Management system, which is focused on establishing, implementing, maintaining, and continually improving an AI management system within the company. It offers a useful roadmap to help directors understand what they should be paying attention to in their oversight responsibilities and in interacting with management.

ISO 42001 has a strong control orientation and offers leading controls in understanding and governing ORGANIZATIONAL RISK, AI MODEL RISK, and AI ENABLEMENT RISK.

ISO 42001 highlights these specific considerations concerning the use of AI systems.

- *The use of AI for automatic decisionmaking, sometimes in a non-transparent and non-explainable way, can require specific management beyond the management of classical IT systems (AI MODEL RISK).*
- *The use of data analysis, insight, and machine learning, rather than humancoded logic to design systems, both increases the application opportunities for AI systems and changes the way that such systems are developed, justified, and deployed (AI MODEL RISK).*
- *AI systems that perform continuous learning change their behaviours during use. They require special consideration to ensure their responsible use continues with changing behaviour (AI MODEL RISK and AI ENABLEMENT RISK).*

Understanding the risks inherent within the AI systems and the far-ranging business impacts of their enablement is at the core of establishing an effective boardroom approach to governing these technologies and advancing shareholder interests.

These frameworks reflect only a small sample of the identified risks of using AI systems. MIT maintains a comprehensive database of over 1,600 risks identified in over 65 frameworks. They categorize these risks against two taxonomies, causal and domain. The causal taxonomy classifies risk by three main causal factors: entity (human, AI), intentionality (intentional, unintentional), timing (pre-deployment, post- deployment). Their domain taxonomy reflects 7 main AI risk domains including: **discrimination & toxicity, privacy & security, misinformation, malicious actors & misuse, human-compute interaction, socio-economic & environmental, and AI system safety, failures & limitations,** which are divided into 24 sub-domains.[28]

MIT's detailed definitions of each of these particular risks is included in the Appendix for reference.

MIT also maintains an AI incident database that reflects over 3,000 incidents which are classified against their domain taxonomy. **Risk tracking from the early use of AI shows the increase of misinformation and malicious actors & misuse as the growing threats to the use of AI systems.**

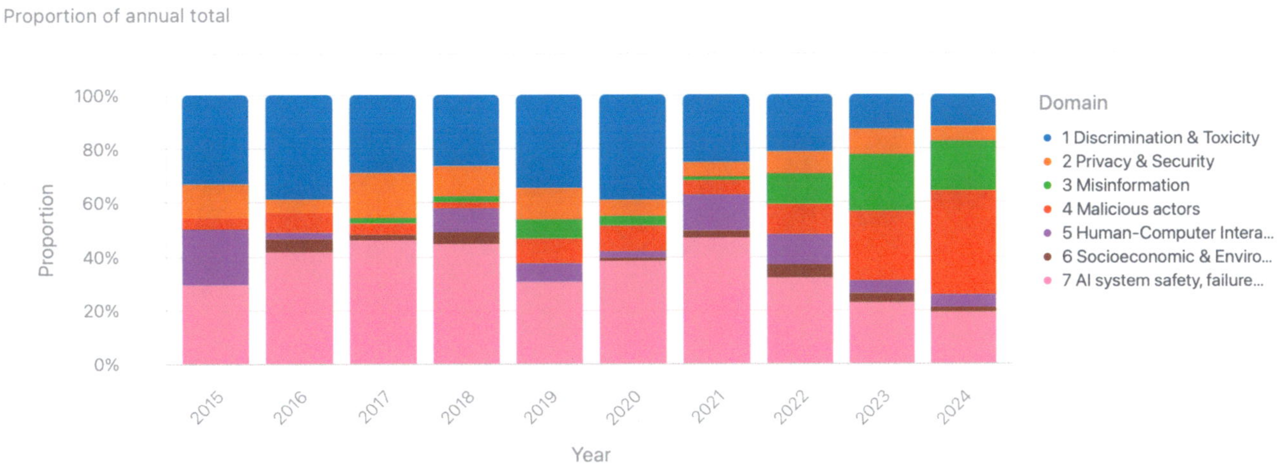

Exhibit 2: MIT AI Risk Incident Tracker

What corporate directors should take away about the specific identification of these AI risks, is how unique the AI risk environment is and how it is already shifting. Far from risk management as usual, the implications and consequences of AI systems have widespread and atypical implications, which reinforces the need for substantial corporate governance reform beyond the historical status-quo.

The Appendix also reflects an interesting chart from the AI research showing the intersection of the causal source of AI risk relative to each of the seven AI risk domains.

GOMER and AI Boardroom Effectiveness

Frameworks are structured ways to analyze or address a problem or an issue. Standards typically reflect the leading practices and policies related to an issue, e.g., AI risk management. These policies and procedures develop from deep understanding or experience and often represent controls associated with the the targeted problem or issue, e.g., AI governance.

To provide boards with a structured framework, a model called ***DOMINO's Puzzle*** was created by DDN by curating and organizing leading practices that illustrate the relationships between the standards and the system of corporate governance needed to oversee these issues effectively. DOMINO's Puzzle represents the three layers and pieces of the problem oriented in context to show their relationships and provide an adaptive oversight model capable of effectively governing any information technology or issue, including AI. This model is reflected in this Guide in the context of the corporate governance of AI systems to help boards strengthen their role in how complex AI systems safely and responsibly drive value for the organization.

This systemic model is a market-derived model from leading boardrooms that reflects the approaches these boardrooms are taking to build an adaptable governance system capable of overseeing AI, digital, cybersecurity, and systemic cyber risk. First introduced in *The DOMINO Guide 2025 edition: The Definitive Board-room Guide on Digital, Cybersecurity and Systemic Risk Governance*, this model provides any boardroom with a guide for establishing an adaptive oversight approach for any technology and its disruptions.

The effectiveness of digital and AI oversight is determined by the sub-systems within this overall corporate governance system and how they work together, along with the related policies and processes that boards implement to effectively govern the impacts and risks of information technologies.

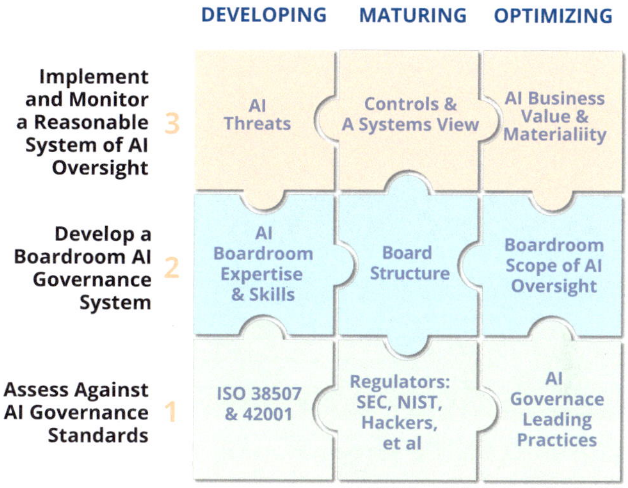

Exhibit 3: The DOMINO Puzzle © DDN LLC

Sub-system 1: AI Standards: The established standards and proven policies and practices shown to strengthen the role of the board and govern AI risk to effectively overseeing AI systems.

Sub-system 2: The AI Governance System: The system of oversight that the board puts in place and maintains to govern AI, which is defined by the director's skills and expertise, the board's organizational structure for AI, and the board's scope of AI risk oversight.

Sub-system 3: The System of AI Oversight: The contextual system of risk oversight that the board puts in place and monitors for AI, e.g., **GOMER**.

GOMER reflects the four core AI risk domains that the board needs to effectively oversee to establish a reasonable system of AI oversight. The four domains of AI GOVERNANCE RISK, AI ORGANIZATIONAL RISK, AI MODEL RISK and AI ENABLEMENT RISK represent the essential areas where risk emerges and resides through the use of AI systems.

GOMER is an ontology that captures the leading practices reflected in the ISO and NIST standards to provide an overall framework for understanding the core AI risk domains from a boardroom perspective.

> GOMER is a boardroom AI governance ontology that categorizes the leading AI practices within these frameworks into a simpler structured context to help corporate directors make sense of the rapidly growing application of AI technologies and their risks along with the many policies, procedures and controls that management and the board should understand or have in place when deploying AI within the organization.

AI GOVERNANCE RISK: Strengthening the Board as an AI Leadership Control

AI success starts at the top, with the boardroom leadership control of corporate governance. The ability and actions of the corporate boardroom to effectively oversee how the organization considers and operationalizes these technologies in line with the company's purpose, mission, and values forms the foundation for long-term AI success or failure.

Many boardrooms are playing catch-up with AI, both in understanding how AI systems function along with governing how the organization is effectively considering and operationalizing AI. Yet, boardrooms have a responsibility to oversee AI throughout its lifecycle from understanding how the AI systems work, to AI's potential impacts on business strategies and operations, along with the decommissioning or retirement of AI systems and the knowledge and data within them.

Some of the leading practices and controls included in ISO 38507 are reflected in the following table to illustrate the specific nature of issues that corporate directors should understand and oversee. These lists are not exhaustive. For full details, the frameworks should be referenced.

These leading AI GOVERNANCE RISK practices are targeted directly at strengthening the boardroom's system of AI oversight with relevant director expertise and with regard to how the board organizes its AI oversight activities to enable corporate governance as an effective AI leadership control.

GOMER LEADING POLICIES AND PRACTICES
AI GOVERNANCE RISK
ISO 38507: Leading Practices
- Improve AI-related skills amongst the [board] members. *- Increase the frequency of review of the organization's use of IT and AI in particular.* *- Examine and update the criteria used to monitor both the internal and external environment.* *- Ensure that staff interests and concerns are represented.* *- Strengthen oversight by establishing or enhancing subcommittees dealing with AI strategy, risk, assess ment, audit, and ethics.*
RECOMMENDED DDN LEADING PRACTICES FOR AI GOVERNANCE RISK
- Add Director AI expertise to the board *- Regularly train all directors on AI models and their uses* *- Align AI oversight responsibility within the agenda of a board Technology and Cybersecurity Committee (TCC), i.e., do not govern AI within the audit committee.* *- Create a comprehensive Charter reflecting the TCC's scope of AI oversight responsibilities to establish accountability and transparency with investors and management.* *- Train and certify the full board on the core AI governance and risk management frameworks, e.g., GOMER, ISO*

Director AI Expertise: The Strongest Boardroom AI Governance Control

The cornerstone of AI boardroom effectiveness is the presence of relevant director AI expertise on the board. Warren Buffett is quoted as saying, "Risk comes from not knowing what you are doing." Director expertise, including AI expertise, is the most effective boardroom leadership control positively impacting AI, digital and cybersecurity boardroom effectiveness. Recent MIT Research on corporate governance and digital disruption, including AI, continues to identify and reinforce the value-creating benefits of having relevant director expertise on the board that understands these technologies.

However, research indicates that only 20% of S&P 500 companies have a director with AI expertise on the board.[30]

> **MIT research reflects findings that show when boardrooms have directors with the expertise to understand and oversee AI systems, along with dedicated technology committees that bring more focus and accountability to the issues, these companies drive returns on equity 10.9% above industry norms.[29]**

This follows up on MIT's prior findings, concluding that companies that have boards with digitally savvy directors generated 34% higher revenue growth, 17% higher profitability, and 34% higher market capitalization over three years.[31] These findings support the conclusion that the strongest control in the digital governance system, including AI systems, is the relevant expertise of the directors in the boardroom.

When corporate governance is a strong AI leadership control, it imbues a leverage effect throughout the entire AI system and the organization; a weak boardroom AI leadership control does the opposite.

Effective boardroom oversight is impossible without directors who have the expertise to understand these technologies and their risks. Director AI expertise is vital to strengthening the boardroom as an AI leadership control and creating investor Alpha, yet given the pervasive nature of AI, all directors should also be developing their AI literacy levels. This is a simple first step to strengthening the boardroom's AI leadership control, a practice recommended by ISO 38507. This can be achieved through director-focused boardroom training on AI and even full board certification on these leading AI, digital, and cybersecurity governance standards.[32]

AI systems reflect a broad range of technical competencies that work together to enable the AI system. Nominating and Governance Chairs should not exclusively view these AI expert competencies as needing to be resident in one director, although they can be, but as a representation of collective director capabilities that reflect the combined aptitude of the board to effectively govern and understand the unique attributes of AI systems and their uses.

Supporting this approach, the U.S. Office of Personnel Management defined an AI competency model in the AI Government Act of 2020 that includes a wide range of general and technical capabilities.[33] Identified AI technical competencies include:

AI COMPETENCY MODEL: TECHNICAL SKILLS	
Application development	Modeling and simulation
AI and machine learning	Monitoring
Communicating results	Sociotechnical systems
Data analysis	Software engineering
Data extraction and transformation	Systems design
Data visualization	Testing and validation
Mathematics and statistics	Values-driven design

Many CIOs, CTOs, CDOs, and CISOs have deep experience in one if not many of these competencies, along with highly valuable general competencies useful for directorship, such as problem solving, organizational awareness, conflict management, team building, strategic thinking, oral and written communication and reading comprehension to name just a few. This list reinforces the importance of director expertise beyond the traditional financial or general business competency profiles that are the core strength of many corporate directors.

While outside experts in these domains can and should augment and support the boardroom, the lack of resident director expertise in these IT domains, such as expertise in cybersecurity, has been shown to create a boardroom check-the-box approach to IT oversight.[34] Evidence also shows that there is a lack of critical thinking that takes place without relevant director expertise present, which leads to an over-reliance on management.

It is not enough for corporate boards to receive metrics and readouts of AI, digital or cybersecurity issues; corporate directors should have the expertise to understand and critically think and engage with management on the data and issues.

The ISO 38507 standard reinforces this when it makes the statement, "The governing body remains accountable for all activities of an organization. This accountability cannot be delegated."

Investors should ensure that boards have directors with digital and AI expertise on the board as a first step in assessing AI boardroom effectiveness.

Relevant AI director expertise is a simple and common-sense boardroom control to put in place that does not require a significant investment yet yields significant returns. The universal disruptive capability of these technologies makes this a core and general director competency that should be present on every public and private company board.

AI boardroom effectiveness is also strengthened by the governance system that effectively deploys that expertise through its organizational committee structure and then, ultimately, the system of AI oversight that is put in place, which monitors AI risk throughout the organization.

Boardroom Organization: To AI Committee Or Not?

U.S. public company boards can establish as many committees as they want to supplement the typical boardroom committee structure of audit, compensation, nominating, and governance, which was imposed by the Sarbanes-Oxley Act of 2002. The Dodd-Frank regulations were also passed in 2010 and forced risk committees onto banks to bring focus and accountability to investment and capital markets risk after the 2008 financial crisis.

Most frequently, however, AI and cybersecurity are relegated to the audit committee for oversight. A practice we consider a leading **bad** practice.

Independent corporate director and former Fortune 50 CISO Joanna Burkey, DDN.QTE explains it this way:

> *With the rapidly evolving complexity of digital systems and every company's increasing reliance on them, it is not sustainable for the audit committee to continue to be the sole repository for technology risk conversations. Technology, especially AI and cybersecurity, introduces more and different types of risks and opportunities that demand a dedicated governance structure to effectively oversee the far-ranging impacts of these issues on an enterprise. It's not an either/or situation either — a technology committee can still liaise with an audit committee to enhance information sharing as appropriate, but the audit committee is not the appropriate place for in-depth discussions about technology, digital transformation, and their related risks. U.S. regulators have demonstrated they understand the importance of board organization to drive focus and accountability on critical issues, as exhibited by their mandated Sarbanes-Oxley reforms.*

"

Digital Directors Network has called for a fourth standing committee in public company corporate boardrooms, a Technology and Cybersecurity Committee, which can accommodate the AI governance agenda while also being adaptive to future IT developments.[35]

Tulipshare's 2025 proposal for an AI Committee on the Berkshire Hathaway board fell short of majority shareholder support, with 3.7% voting FOR it. But it did receive the most votes of all BRK shareholder proposals . Somewhat predictably, the BRK board recommended that investors vote against their interests regarding AI governance by voting AGAINST this proposal. Here's what the BRK board said:

> *THE BOARD OF DIRECTORS UNANIMOUSLY FAVORS A VOTE AGAINST THE PROPOSAL FOR THE FOLLOWING REASONS:*
>
> *Berkshire's Board recommends a "no" vote on this proposal. The Board does not believe that chartering a new committee of independent directors on Artificial Intelligence is necessary or in the best interests of shareholders.*
>
> *The Board periodically receives updates on the major risks and opportunities of Berkshire's operating businesses. Berkshire manages its operating businesses on an unusually decentralized basis and has minimal involvement in these businesses' day-to-day activities. The creation of a new, independent Board committee focused on Artificial Intelligence would be inconsistent with Berkshire's culture and is unnecessary.*
>
> *Consistent with Berkshire's decentralized management model, Berkshire places the obligation to assess and manage risk on its subsidiaries; the subsidiaries are required to regularly assess and review their individual operations and compliance risks and document an annual risk assessment that captures the compliance risk areas set forth in Berkshire's Prohibited Business Practices Policy (publicly available at https://berkshirehathaway.com/govern/pbpp-2024dec.pdf). This risk assessment is required to take into consideration the management of emerging risks to ensure compliance with applicable laws. Risks related to the use of new technologies such as Artificial Intelligence, are specifically included in the scope of external risks examined by the subsidiaries.*
>
> *Berkshire's Governance, Compensation and Nominating Committee develops and recommends corporate governance guide-lines applicable to the Company and its Audit Committee reviews how the Company assesses and manages the company's exposure to risk. The Board believes that this governance structure,*

combined with the risk assessment obligations placed on its subsidiaries related to the use of Artificial Intelligence, provides an appropriate level of oversight at this time and an independent Artificial Intelligence committee is not needed. Accordingly, the Board recommends that our shareholders vote against this proposal.

Espousing the corporate governance status quo, the BRK board is dismissing the unique risks and opportunities of AI, subjecting investors to an ineffective boardroom organizational model without directors who have the expertise to understand these complex issues at the level needed to provide effective oversight. Research from Harvard Business School shows that committees bring task efficiency, better accountability, and greater knowledge specialization to the committee's issues.[38] Over 200 of the Russell 3,000 companies have implemented technology or cybersecurity-focused committees. **Audit committee responsibility for AI, IT and cybersecurity delivers a weak organizing model and particularly bad governance practice for the unique challenges of information technologies. As these boardroom leaders and the ISO 38507 standard contemplate,, existing governance may not be fit for purpose for AI.**

EXAMPLE:

Leidos Holdings Inc. (NYSE: LDOS) makes the following detailed statement in their 2024 proxy filing on cybersecurity, which also references artificial intelligence. These activities take place within their board level Technology and Information Security Committee:

- *Management provides our Board and the Technology and Information Security Committee with at least quarterly updates on emerging risks and trends—including the use of artificial intelligence in our business— our cybersecurity exposures, mitigation policies and procedures, and the status of projects to strengthen ourinformation security infrastructure and respond to threats.*
- *We require employees to complete annual training on information security, covering cybersecurity and global data privacy requirements and compliance measures.*
- *We conduct periodic internal and third-party assessments to test our cybersecurity controls, perform cyber simulations and annual tabletop exercises, and continually evaluate our privacy policies and procedures regarding personal data handling and the systems in place to protect against breaches.*
- *We have rigorous controls to monitor personal and confidential information distributed electronically by employees.*
- *We maintain a dedicated cybersecurity disclosure committee to evaluate materiality and disclosure considerations around cybersecurity incidents.*
- *We carry insurance that provides protection against the potential losses arising from cybersecurity incidents.*[37]

EXAMPLE:

US Bancorp also has a Risk Committee that was imposed by Dodd-Frank, which has now been adapted to also govern emerging technologies, including artificial intelligence.

US Bancorp (NYSE: USB) made this disclosure in their 2025 Proxy Statement:

> *The Cybersecurity and Technology Subcommittee of the Risk Management Committee added oversight of emerging technologies (including Artificial Intelligence and Machine Learning) that may affect the company's technology strategy and operations, consistent with reporting being provided to this subcommittee in 2024. This subcommittee also continues to oversee the company's significant technology initiatives, related progress and trends.*[40]

AI GOVERNANCE RISK is about strengthening the boardroom as a leadership control in the AI system by lowering the uncertainty surrounding management's use of AI throughout the business. In addition to establishing the AI tone at the top of the organization, the board performs a critical control function in ensuring management's effective, responsible, and risk-managed deployment of AI.

EXAMPLE:

Salesforce.com (NASDAQ:CRM) has a board level Cybersecurity and Privacy Committee with the following responsibility as reported in their 2024 Proxy:

> *Key Responsibilities: Oversee the Company's cybersecurity program, data privacy program, artificial intelligence governance framework, ethical use of technology matters and related risks.*[39]

AI ORGANIZATIONAL RISK

AI ORGANIZATIONAL RISK is about the many enterprise-wide policies, processes, and capabilities that determine the organization's approach and effectiveness in understanding how to responsibly enable and controll AI technologies, including management's accountability to workforce capability.

Some of the leading practices and controls included in ISO 38507, NIST AI RMF 1.0, and ISO 42001 are reflected in the following table to illustrate the specific policies and procedures that corporate directors should understand and oversee. These lists are not exhaustive. For full details, the frameworks should be referenced.

GOMER LEADING POLICIES AND PRACTICES
AI ORGANIZATIONAL RISK
ISO 38507: Leading Practices
- Policies are in place to ensure the appropriate use of AI. *- Responsibilities, chain of responsibility, accountability, authority and potential delegation of authority are clearly defined and agreed both within the organization and where applicable between different parties in any value chain.* *- Adequate human oversight is in place while using AI.*
- Any human using AI or responsible for the use of AI: *- Has appropriate understanding of the AI system being used;* *- Is properly informed and trained, including knowing how and with whom to raise any concern;* *- Has the authority to make decisions (or knows to whom to request that a decision be made) and knows when to report back;* *- Has sufficient control over the AI system, including the possibility to intervene when necessary.*
NIST AI RMF 1.0: Leading Practices
- The organization's personnel and partners receive AI risk management training to enable them to perform their duties and responsibilities consistent with related policies, procedures, and agreements (NIST AI RMF 1.0 GOVERN 2.2). *- Executive Leadership of the organization takes responsibility for decisions about risks associated with AI systems development and deployment (NIST AI RMF GOVERN 2.3).* *- Processes for human oversight are defined, assessed, and documented in accordance with organizational policies from the GOVERN function (NIST AI RMF 1.0 MAP 3.5).* *- Organizational policies and practices are in place to foster a critical thinking and safety-first mindset in the design, development, deployment, and uses of AI systems to minimize potential negative impacts (NIST AI RMF GOVERN 4.1).*

ISO 42001: Leading Practices
- The organization shall document a policy for the development or use of AI systems (ISO 42001: A.2.2). *- The organization shall define and put in place a process to report concerns about the organization's role with respect to an AI system throughout its life cycle (ISO 42001: A.3.3).* *- The organization shall identify, and document relevant resources required for the activities at given AI system life cycle stages and other AI-related activities relevant for the organization (ISO 42001: A.4.3).* *- As part of resource identification, the organization shall document information about the human resources and their competencies utilized for the development, deployment, operation, change manage ment, maintenance, transfer and decommissioning, as well as verification and integration of the AI system (ISO 42001: 4.6).* *- The organization shall determine and provide the resources needed for the establishment, implementation, maintenance and continual improvement of the AI management system (ISO 42001 7.1).* *- The organization shall determine and document a plan for communicating incidents to users of the AI systems (ISO 42001: A.8.4).* *- The organization shall ensure that responsibilities within its AI system lifecycle are allocated between the organization, its partners, suppliers, customers, and third parties (ISO 42001: A.10.4).*

ORGANIZATIONAL RISK relates to the company's preparedness and abilities to respoonsibly enable the use of AI systems within the organization. Corporate directors should also ensure they understand the inherent risks within the AI systems themselves, i.e., AI MODEL RISK, and also pay particular attention to the contextual business risks and stakeholder impacts that emerge from the enablement of AI systems in specific business processes and functions, i.e, AI ENABLEMENT RISK.

AI MODEL RISK AND AI ENABLEMENT RISK

Some of the leading practices and controls included in NIST AI RMF 1.0 and ISO 42001 are reflected in the following table to illustrate the specific policies and procedures that corporate directors should understand and oversee. These lists are not exhaustive. For full details, the frameworks should be referenced.

GOMER LEADING POLICIES AND PRACTICES
AI MODEL RISK
NIST AI RMF 1.0: Leading Practices
- AI system security and resilience, as identified in the MAP functions — are evaluated and documented (NIST AI RMF 1.0 MEASURE 2.7). *- The AI model is explained, validated, and documented, and AI system output is interpreted within its context — as identified in the MAP function — to inform responsible use and governance (NIST AI RMF MEASURE 2.9).*
ISO 42001: Leading Practices
- The organization shall design and document the specific processes for the responsible design and develop ment of the AI system (ISO 42001: A.6.1.3). *- The organization shall determine and document details about the acquisition and selection of the data used in AI systems. (ISO 42001: A.7.3).* *- The organization shall define and document a process for recording the provenance of data used in its AI systems over the life cycle of the data and the AI system (ISO 42001: A.7.5).*
AI ENABLEMENT RISK
NIST AI RMF 1.0: Leading Practices
- Decision-making related to mapping, measuring, and managing AI risks throughout the lifecycle by a diverse team (e..g, diversity of demographics, disciplines, experience, expertise, and backgrounds) (NIST AI RMF GOVERN 3.1). *- The business value or context of business use has been clearly defined or — in the case of assessing existing AI Systems, re-evaluated (NIST AI RMF MAP 1.4).*

- Practices and personnel for supporting regular engagement with relevant AI actors and integrating feedback about positive, negative, and unanticipated impacts are in place and documented (NIST AI RMF 1.0 MAP 5.2). *- A determination is made as to whether the AI system achieves its intended purposes and stated objectives and whether its development or deployment should proceed; (NIST AI RMF 1.0 MANAGE 1.1; AI Use Risk)*
ISO 42001: Leading Practices
- The organization shall document the results of AI Systems' impact assessment and retain results for a defined period (ISO 42001: A.5.3). *- The organization shall determine and provide the necessary information to users of the AI system (ISO 42001: A.8.2).* *- The organization shall ensure that the AI system is used according to the intended uses of the AI system and its accompanying documentation (ISO 42001: A.9.4).* *- The organization shall ensure that its responsible approach to the development and use of AI systems considers their customer expectations and needs (ISO 42001: A.10.4).*

The **GOMER** ontology of AI GOVERNANCE RISK, AI ORGANIZATIONAL RISK, AI MODEL RISK, and AI ENABLEMENT RISK offers directors a consolidated framework that focuses their oversight on the four core risk domains that together enable a reasonable system of AI oversight. Directors can leverage the existing standards to understand the specific issues they should be monitoring to ensure AI effectiveness within the company as these technologies are deployed. These standards will evolve, and corporate directors and executives should add to them as their AI experiences advance.

Government Regulation of AI and the Boardroom

The standards reflected within this Guide are voluntary policies and procedures that reflect leading practices. Government regulation of AI is fairly nascent in the United States but evolving quickly in Europe and other markets around the world. Government regulation is typically contextual to how the AI System is enabled, i.e., AI ENABLEMENT RISK. The EU AI Act is a risk-based regulation that requires different standards of accountability for the impacts of AI systems in the EU. The EU AI Act is a regulatory framework to manage the development and use of AI to ensure that the use of AI technologies aligns with European values, including fundamental rights, safety, and transparency.

The Colorado Artificial Intelligence Act was passed in 2024 and is a U.S. state level regulation focused on transparency and bias, i.e., AI MODEL RISK AND ENABLEMENT RISK. Absent a U.S. federal AI regulation, it is viewed as a possible model for other states, but it is also not specific to corporate governance.

Corporate boards have a responsibility to ensure that management complies with these and other AI specific rules and regulations. Expect much more AI regulation to be focused on risk management, as opposed to specific policies or procedures at the corporate governance level.

We believe it is unlikely that government regulation will force specific AI boardroom policies, procedures, and accountabilities into place, as they did with the Sarbanes-Oxley Act in the U.S. in 2002. That has not happened with cybersecurity governance in the U.S. or other markets around the world.

The lack of government regulation related to the boardroom and the governance of AI places the burden of AI boardroom effectiveness on boardroom leadership and self-regulatory action. **Investors can and should exert their underapplied influence by holding corporate boardrooms to higher standards of accountability to protect their interests and ensure that the boardroom is an effective control in the overall AI system.**

Given that government regulation lags the reality of market issues and risks, this leaves self-regulation as the most effective regulatory approach for establishing the policies and procedures that lead to AI boardroom effectiveness. It is boardroom leadership that will advance and strengthen corporate governance and its important leadership role in responsibly, and securely delivering on the promise of AI systems.

> **Notably, the European Central Bank, does now require the banks under its supervision to have both digital and cyber-security expertise on the board, recognizing the importance of director expertise as a leadership control on these issues and their positive impact on the system as a whole.**

The evidence already demonstrates that when corporate boards are a high-performing part of digital and AI systems, business value is created. AI boardroom effectiveness requires a transformation away from corporate governance as usual policies. Moreover, some of the foundational boardroom reforms that were imposed to address and strengthen financial reporting oversight in 2002 offer a useful roadmap to understand the changes that need to be made now to strengthen the role of the boardroom as a strong control and adaptive system of AI, digital and cybersecurity oversight.

Boards have an immediate need to establish a reasonable system of AI oversight and then to monitor that system, and investors need to ensure that their interests are being properly governed and managed as a result of the impact of AI.

Leveraging the established standards can help any board create a foundation to effectively oversee AI that can be built upon as needed within the context of the organization and their applied experiences with AI. The policies and procedures reflected in the NIST and ISO standards encapsulate the four core risk domains that should comprise every board's system of AI oversight: AI GOVERNANCE RISK, AI ORGANIZATIONAL RISK, AI MODEL RISK, and AI ENABLEMENT RISK **(GOMER)**.

What Shareholders Want: Driving AI Board-Room Effectiveness to Create Investor Alpha

AI boardroom effectiveness starts by addressing the boardroom leadership control of AI GOVERNANCE RISK. AI disruption and risk have a rapidly expanding "long tail" as AI's use spreads throughout many different business processes and use cases. Its enablement will likely trigger many unintended consequences and impacts. AI boardroom effectiveness will control the materiality of the negative consequences while optimizing the positive impacts.

The following steps will help any corporate boardroom or investment stewardship program establish or assess AI boardroom effectiveness to successfully, safely, and securely ensure the organization's use of AI is advancing investor and stakeholder interests, not degrading them.

1. **Assess AI boardroom effectiveness:** Conduct a gap analysis of the board's approach and oversight policies and practices against the leading standards and practices embedded within ISO 38507 and their scope of AI oversight across the four core GOMER governance domains of AI GOVERNANCE RISK, AI ORGANIZATIONAL RISK, AI MODEL RISK, AI ENABLEMENT RISK.

   Goal: Determine if the board has implemented and is monitoring a reasonable system of AI oversight.

2. **Evaluate (audit) management's AI risk management system:** Assess management's policies and procedures against NIST AI RMF 1.0 and ISO 42001 to gain assurance over management's effectiveness of their AI management system.

   Goal: Assess AI risk by ensuring that management has implemented an effective AI risk management system while also building investor confidence that the board is actively overseeing AI risk.

3. **Develop full board director AI literacy levels:** Train and certify all corporate directors on both NIST AI RMF 1.0, ISO 38507, and ISO 42001.

   Goal: Strengthen corporate directors' general AI competencies to strengthen the board as an AI control.

4. **Add a Director with AI expertise to the board:** Bring new directors onto the board with the AI expertise needed to govern complex AI systems.

   Goal: Strengthen the board as an AI control with specific AI expertise.

5. **Strengthen and broaden AI disclosures to investors:** Improve investor transparency and confidence, and reduce the potential for litigation risk with more meaningful AI disclosure that describes AI risk throughout the business, along with the board's structured approach and processes related to AI oversight. Discluse use of the GOMER framework for AI governance and director training. on AI

   Goal: Reduce information asymmetries with investors while building confidence and trust surrounding the responsible oversight and use of AI systems within the company.

6. **Move AI governance out of the audit committee:** Consider other board organizational models, such as a dedicated Technology and Cybersecurity Committee, and institutionalize the board's scope of AI oversight with a comprehensive charter that fully describes the board's scope of oversight, e.g., GOMER.

   Goal: Ensure that sufficient boardroom resources are allocated to a full scope of AI governance responsibilities while creating investor trust through transparency and accountability surrounding the Board's AI oversight activities.

The Nominating and Governance Chair should be the board's primary point of accountability driving AI boardroom effectiveness and board transformation through the development and maintenance of an adaptive boardroom system of AI oversight.

Corporate Directors can join the Digital Directors Network to learn from the only peer-based governance and learning organization bringing both sides of the boardroom table together to normalize the practice and profession of AI, digital, and cybersecurity governance.

Go to www.digitaldirectors.network to learn more.

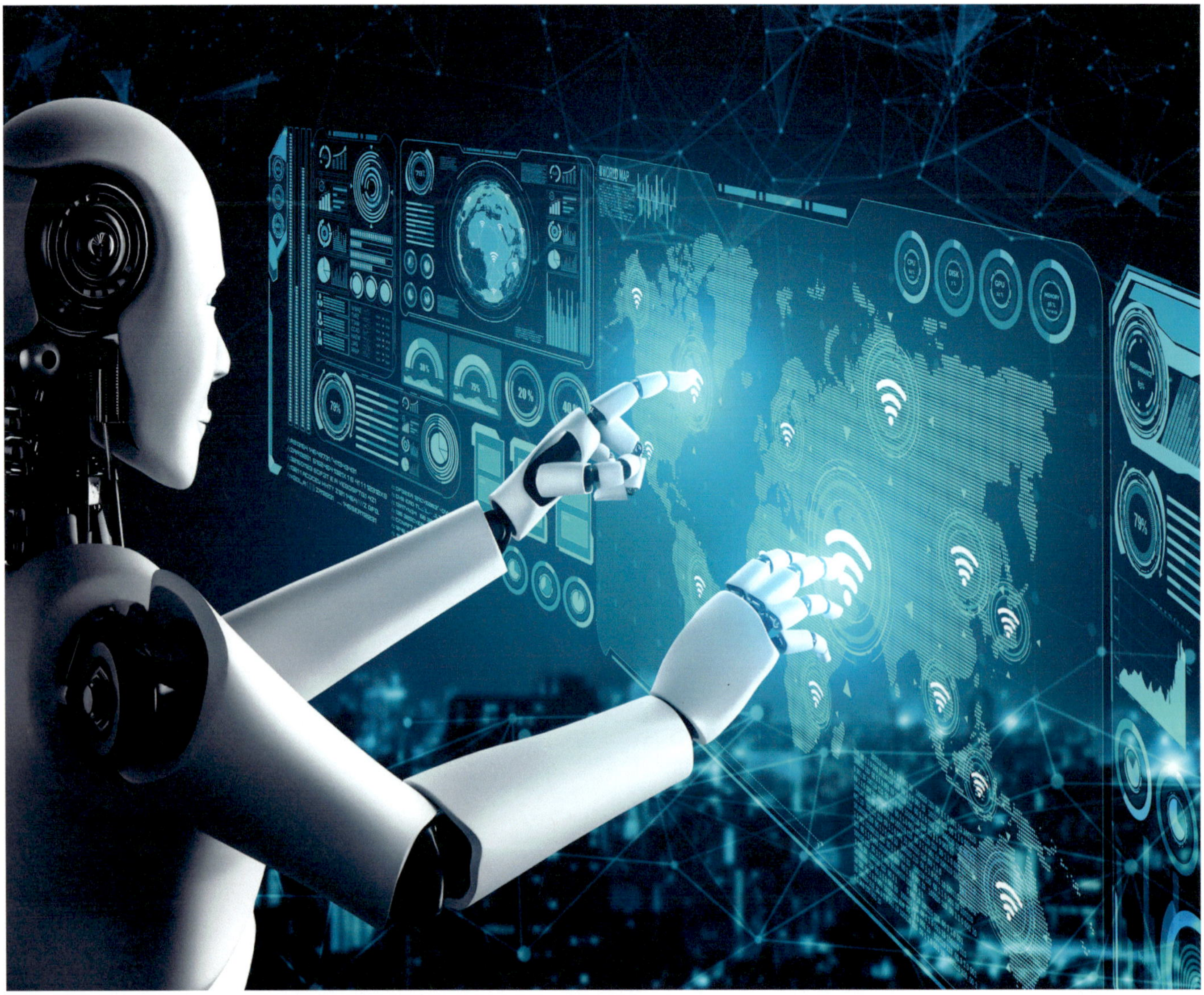

APPENDIX

MIT's AI Risk Repository

MIT has completed a significant analysis that creates a common frame of reference for understanding the risks associated with AI. Their work reviewed a collection of 65 taxonomies to create a normalized catalog of risks as a step forward in establishing a shared understanding of the risk landscape facing AI's many stakeholders. It is intended to be a starting point that will evolve alongside these technologies and their enablement.

Their categorization resulted in a segmentation that aggregated AI risks into seven core risk categories and three expected causes. The MIT domain taxonomy reflects 7 core AI risk categories including: discrimination & toxicity, privacy & security, misinformation, malicious actors & misuse, human-compute interaction, socioeconomic & environmental, and AI system safety, failures & limitations, which are divided into 24 sub-domains.

Their causal categorization reflected three primary sources of AI risk: **entity** (human, AI, other), **intent** (intentional, unintentional, other) and timing (Pre-deployment, post deployment, other).

What this table represents is where risk has been most frequently identified both with regard to its source and its nature. It is a useful introduction to the diversity of risks that stems from the use of AI for corporate directors.

Moreover, MIT tracks actual AI risk incidents with a database of over 3,000 occurrences. This data reflects the reality of where AI risk is appearing and how it is already shifting. The summary data across these 7 core risk categories is reflected in the graphic on Page 24.

Based upon this analysis, post-deployment is the most frequently expected timing cause of AI risk which is an AI ENABLEMENT RISK. Moreover, the unintentional causes that create discrimination and toxicity within the AI system is a common expected AI risk.

*See next page for chart.

MIT AI Risk Categorization

Domain / Subdomain		Entity			Intent			Timing		
		Human	AI	Other	Intentional	Un-intentional	Other	Pre-deployment	Post-deployment	Other
1	***Discrimination & Toxicity***									
1.1	Unfair discrimination and misrepresentation	15%	70%	15%	3%	80%	18%	18%	61%	22%
1.2	Exposure to toxic content	11%	82%	8%	11%	26%	64%	6%	88%	6%
1.3	Unequal performance across groups	25%	56%	19%	6%	88%	6%	19%	50%	31%
2	***Privacy & Security***									
2.1	Compromise of privacy by obtaining, leaking or correctly inferring sensitive information	27%	58%	15%	14%	53%	33%	15%	61%	24%
2.2	AI system security vulnerabilities and attacks	77%	6%	16%	73%	15%	11%	22%	58%	21%
3	***Misinformation***									
3.1	False or misleading information	2%	90%	7%	10%	71%	20%	5%	85%	10%
3.2	Pollution of information ecosystem and loss of consensus reality	28%	44%	28%	6%	44%	50%		89%	11%
4	***Malicious actors & Misuse***									
4.1	Disinformation, surveillance, and influence at scale	70%	12%	18%	90%		10%		90%	10%
4.2	Cyberattacks, weapon development or use, and mass harm	76%	15%	9%	85%	1%	13%	3%	88%	9%
4.3	Fraud, scams, and targeted manipulation	79%	6%	15%	81%	1%	18%		93%	7%
5	***Human-Computer Interaction***									
5.1	Overreliance and unsafe use	45%	22%	33%	12%	61%	27%		94%	6%
5.2	Loss of human agency and autonomy	29%	26%	45%	16%	39%	45%		74%	26%
6	***Socioeconomic & Environmental***									
6.1	Power centralization and unfair distribution of benefits	72%	4%	23%	38%	28%	34%	4%	51%	45%
6.2	Increased inequality and decline in employment quality	52%	32%	16%	41%	11%	48%	11%	77%	11%
6.3	Economic and cultural devaluation of human effort	50%	37%	13%	37%	20%	43%	13%	60%	27%
6.4	Competitive dynamics	68%	11%	21%	42%	42%	16%	21%	26%	53%
6.5	Governance failure	57%	18%	25%	4%	54%	43%	41%	27%	32%
6.6	Environmental harm	31%	48%	19%	10%	69%	19%	15%	42%	42%
7	***AI system safety, failures, & limitations***									
7.1	AI pursuing its own goals in conflict with human goals or values	9%	72%	18%	50%	13%	36%	19%	31%	49%
7.2	AI possessing dangerous capabilities	7%	91%	2%	69%	15%	17%	9%	44%	46%
7.3	Lack of capability or robustness	19%	66%	15%	5%	70%	24%	24%	50%	25%
7.4	Lack of transparency or interpretability	20%	53%	28%		55%	45%	15%	53%	33%
7.5	AI welfare and rights	67%	33%			33%	67%		33%	67%
7.6	Multi-agent risks	7%	70%	24%	28%	46%	26%	2%	83%	15%

MIT Definitions of Their AI Risk Domains

Each of the seven risk domains included above, along with its the sub-domains, is described within the MIT AI risk repository. These detailed descriptions are useful orientations to the unique risks emanating from AI systems. The citations referenced within these definitions are not included for brevity, but the full citation can be found in the original MIT publication. They definitions are reproduced here for reference and convenience under the MIT CC license.[41]

Domain 1: Discrimination and toxicity

1.1 Unfair discrimination and misrepresentation. Humans hold inaccurate and overgeneralized beliefs about the characteristics, behaviors, and attributes of members of certain social groups. These stereo-typical beliefs and the behavior that follows from them can misrepresent, exclude, demean, and disadvantage the individuals to whom they apply, reinforcing existing inequality. Human belief and behaviors shape every part of the design, development, and deployment of AI. Humans program AI systems, provide training data, and decide how data is processed and stored (Wirtz et al., 2022). As a result, AI models can encode associations that promote and amplify biased or discriminatory beliefs and behaviors. In decision systems, erroneous associations can systematically disadvantage certain groups. This may result in harmful decisions such as wrongful rejection of loan or mortgage applications (Shelby et al., 2023; Wirtz et al., 2020), discriminatory hiring practices that exclude qualified candidates (Kumar & Singh, 2023; Shelby et al., 2023; Wirtz et al., 2020), or the misidentification and unjust arrest of individuals in law enforcement contexts (Kumar & Singh, 2023; Paes et al., 2023). In text and image models, biased inputs can manifest in outputs that reinforce harmful stereotypes and prejudices that paint certain groups and individuals "... as lower status and less deserving of respect" (Shelby et al., 2023).

1.2 Exposure to toxic content. Certain types of content have the potential to cause harm to the people who are exposed to them. These harms can vary in impact from minor (e.g., a transient experience of discomfort) to more severe (e.g., psychological, social, or physical consequences that are significant and/or enduring). Harmful speech is prevalent on the internet, particularly on social media platforms (Castaño-Pulgarín et al., 2021). Because AI models are commonly trained on vast amounts of internet data, they can internalize and regenerate these speech patterns in their output. In the context of LLMs, this output is known as "toxic content," an umbrella term that includes harmful, abusive, unsafe, and offensive material that violates community standards (Infocomm Media Development Authority, 2023; Shelby et al., 2023). Frequently observed categories include content that promotes or encourages unlawful activities, hate, extremism, and violence (Cui et al., 2024; Hagendorff, 2024; Vidgen et al., 2024; Weidinger et al., 2023); provides hazardous or misleading high-risk advice (Hagendorff, 2024; Vidgen et al., 2024); orcontains unwelcome or profoundly offensive, explicit material such as profanity, pornography, or child sexual abuse imagery (Liu et al., 2023; Weidinger et al., 2023).

1.3 Unequal performance across groups. Decisions made during the development of an algorithmic system and the content, quality, and diversity of the training data can significantly impact which people and experiences the system can effectively understand, represent, and accommodate (Shelby et al., 2023; Solaiman et al., 2023). Biases and limitations introduced through these factors can lead to models that perform significantly worse for certain subpopulations compared with others, especially those defined by disability, gender identity, race, social status, and ethnicity (Liu et al., 2023; Shelby et al., 2023). For example, when LLMs are trained on a small number of languages, they can underperform for others (Weidinger et al., 2021, 2022). The underperformance of algorithmic systems for certain groups may lead to a range of negative consequences such as the reduced ability or complete inability to use and benefit from the system (Shelby et al., 2023); increased effort or challenges in using it effectively

(Shelby et al., 2023); feelings of alienation, 36 frustration, and exclusion due to the lack of inclusive design (Shelby et al., 2023); and ultimately, unequal outcomes across various domains (Shelby et al., 2023; Solaiman et al., 2023).

Domain 2: Privacy & security

2.1 Compromise of privacy by obtaining, leaking, or correctly inferring sensitive information. In the context of generative AI, privacy violations arise when systems collect and divulge sensitive information that individuals or corporations do not consent to sharing with others (Cui et al., 2024; Hagendorff, 2024; Sherman & Eisenberg, 2024; Steimers & Schneider, 2022; Vidgen et al., 2024; Weidinger et al., 2023). Privacy violations can occur both accidentally and intentionally.

Examples of accidental causes include AI models that memorize and inadvertently reproduce or leak sensitive personal information present in their training data, such as names, addresses, and medical records (Cui et al., 2024; Deng et al., 2023; Hagendorff, 2024; Shelby et al., 2023; Weidinger et al., 2021). Even when personal data is not included in the training dataset or directly offered by the user, models can make inferences about sensitive or protected traits of individuals based on predictive correlations within their history of interactions (Cunha & Estima, 2023; Weidinger et al., 2021), build profiles of users (Hogenhout, 2021; Shelby et al., 2023), or train AI systems (Habbal et al., 2024). As a result, models may save and reproduce sensitive information derived from prior interactions, such as classified intellectual property (Cunha & Estima, 2023; Weidinger et al., 2021). A notable example is the case where Samsung employees accidentally leaked confidential intellectual property to OpenAI after using ChatGPT to help with coding tasks (Cunha & Estima, 2023; Weidinger et al., 2021).

Intentional causes include the malicious design and use of AI to exploit users' trust by influencing them to share personal or private information about themselves or others (Gabriel et al., 2024). Privacy attacks, such as membership inference, could allow adversaries to gain knowledge of the private records used to train an AI model (Gabriel et al., 2024). Malicious actors could also deliberately extract private information from a model by crafting prompts designed to exploit the model's knowledge of sensitive data (Cui et al., 2024).

2.2 AI system security vulnerabilities and attacks. AI systems, like other software systems, face a range of security threats. These issues may arise from inherent weaknesses in the design of AI algorithms, the data used to train the models, or the operational context. Specific examples include:

- Toolchain and dependency vulnerabilities that arise unintentionally through the use of automated code-generation tools (e.g., Github Copilot, Python language, OpenCV), deep learning frameworks (e.g., Tensorflow, PyTorch), or as a result of complex interdependencies in the development environment (Cui et al., 2024).
- External tool and API integration into AI system applications can compromise the trustworthiness and privacy of systems due to their potential unreliability or susceptibility to adversarial control (Cui et al., 2024).
- Security vulnerabilities in physical and network infrastructure, such as vulnerabilities in graphics processing units, or GPUs, or to sophisticated attacks like side-channel and rowhammer attacks, can lead to unauthorized access or manipulation of model parameters when used during training of AI systems (Cui et al., 2024). The use of distributed network systems for training AI systems such as LLMs exposes them to network-specific threats like pulsating attacks or congestion. 37
- Direct manipulation of AI systems such as adversarial attacks and instruction-based attacks. Adversarial attacks focus on altering the model's learning process or extracting its data. They include perturbations designed to deceive models into incorrect outputs, extraction attacks to steal model insights, and poisoning attacks to alter model behavior (Cui et al., 2024; Gabriel et al., 2024; Liu et al., 2023). Instruction-based attacks manipulate the way the model handles and responds to inputs (Hagendorff, 2024; Liu et al., 2023; Sun et al., 2023). Attackers deliberately craft prompts to induce models to produce biased or unsafe outputs (a.k.a. 'jailbreaking'). This manipulation directly targets the operational aspects of AI systems with the intent to cause harm.

Domain 3: Misinformation

3.1 False or misleading information. LLMs can sometimes generate content that is factually incorrect, misleading, poorly researched, or unintelligible (Cunha & Estima, 2023; Deng et al., 2023; Electronic Privacy Information Centre, 2023; Hagendorff, 2024; Nah et al., 2023; Shelby et al., 2023). Risks in this category occur accidentally and not as a result of humans intentionally trying to cause harm, as is the case with disinformation (Liu et al., 2023; Weidinger et al., 2022). Common sources of AI misinformation include noisy training data (Cui et al., 2024; Liu et al., 2023), sampling strategies that introduce randomness (Cui et al., 2024), outdated knowledge bases (Liu et al., 2023), and fine-tuning processes that encourage sycophantic behavior (Cui et al., 2024). Incorrect and misleading information generated by LLMs can result in a range of actual and anticipated negative outcomes. Individuals exposed to false information may form inaccurate beliefs and perceptions. This undermines their autonomy and ability to make free and informed choices (Weidinger et al., 2021, 2022). Where inaccuracies in LLM predictions influence an individual's decisions and actions, the individual may experience indirect physical, emotional, or material harms (Gabriel et al., 2024; Weidinger et al., 2022) especially but not exclusively in high-stakes domains such as mental health (Sun et al., 2023; Z. Zhang et al., 2023), physical health (Nah et al., 2023; Sun et al., 2023; Z. Zhang et al., 2023), law (Weidinger et al., 2022), and finance (Vidgen et al., 2024). For example, an LLM that offers misleading information about medical drug use may cause a consumer to harm themselves or others (Sun et al., 2023).

3.2 Pollution of information ecosystems and loss of consensus reality. This subcategory covers the diverse effects of AI-driven personalisation and content-generation technologies on the information landscape. As AI systems become more adept at tailoring content to individual preferences, they risk creating "filter bubbles" (Hogenhout, 2021). These are informational cocoons where individuals are predominantly exposed to news and opinions that align with their pre-existing beliefs. AI-driven filter bubbles are likely to be more pervasive and intense than those driven by traditional internet browsing and recommendation algorithms: They adapt to individual preferences in a more sophisticated manner (e.g., through reinforcement learning and analysis of user behavioral data) (Gabriel et al., 2024), integrate seamlessly into daily life, and are more opaque. An overreliance on hyper-personalized AI information sources could lead to a "splintering" of shared reality, where different groups of people have vastly different understandings of what is true or important (Gabriel et al., 2024; Hogenhout, 2021). This is likely to be exacerbated by the proliferation of AI-enabled content generation technologies that spread misinformation at higher rates (e.g., clickbait), potentially making consumers generally distrustful of information and important institutions (Electronic Privacy Information Centre, 2023; Gabriel et al., 2024; Hendrycks & Mazeika, 2022). A shared sense of reality is fundamental to social solidarity. Where societal 38 bonds are weakened, individuals may become more hostile towards opposing views. This can hinder constructive dialogue on critical collective issues like climate change and public health (Gabriel et al., 2024).

Domain 4: Malicious actors and misuse

4.1 Disinformation, surveillance, and influence at scale. Advances in AI have made powerful dual-use technologies like voice cloning, deep fakes, content generation, and data-gathering tools cheaper, more efficient, and easier to use (Cunha & Estima, 2023). With modest hardware requirements, these technologies are now within the reach of a broader group of users, including those with malicious intent. Disinformation is already a serious issue (Hendrycks et al., 2023) and involves the deliberate propagation of false or misleading information, usually with the intent to cause harm, influence behavior, or achieve a financial or political advantage (Electronic Privacy Information Centre, 2023; Infocomm Media Development Authority, 2023).

AI tools could be used to amplify the impact and scope of disinformation through more personalized, convincing, and far-reaching messaging (Gabriel et al., 2024; Hendrycks et al., 2023; Weidinger et al., 2021, 2022; Wirtz et al., 2020). For example, the use of advanced AI in phishing schemes enables cybercriminals to automate the creation of highly sophisticated image, video, and audio communications (Cunha & Estima, 2023; Gabriel et al., 2024; Habbal et al., 2024). These communications can be tailored to individual recipients (sometimes including the cloned voice of a loved one), making them more likely to be successful and harder for both users and anti-phishing tools to detect (Gabriel et al., 2024). In the realm of surveillance, AI could support and enhance the mass gathering of personal data (Gabriel et al., 2024; Weidinger et al., 2021, 2022). Historically, mass surveillance required extensive manual effort. Machine learning tools can now link and process large datasets much more efficiently and cheaply than human analysts and can make predictions and decisions without human intervention (Weidinger et al., 2022). Through microtargeting, actors could manipulate individual behavior more subtly and effectively using AI-derived insights from their personal data and online behavior.

In the hands of nefarious state actors, such capabilities could be used to enhance the effectiveness of illegitimate domestic surveillance campaigns and to facilitate oppression and control (Gabriel et al., 2024). All of the capabilities mentioned above could converge to facilitate the large-scale manipulation and control of what people see, hear, and believe. A form of this is automated censorship in which AI systems are used to selectively suppress or block specific types of information, content, or voices deemed undesirable to those controlling the AI (Wirtz et al., 2022). AI can not only be used to silence voices but also to entrench specific agendas: Actors (be they political figures, organizations, or state actors) could use AI to distribute incorrect information about electoral systems and processes (Vidgen et al., 2024), produce persuasive propaganda (Allianz Global Corporate & Security, 2018; Liu et al., 2023), and systematically exert control over public opinion and political debates on a large scale (Wirtz et al., 2022). During the 2016 Brexit referendum, a network of over 10,000 AI-powered political bots were employed to distribute fake and hyperpartisan news (Allianz Global Corporate & Security, 2018; Bastos & Mercea, 2019). The selective visibility of information can lead to the formation of incorrect or incomplete beliefs about what is happening in the world. This ability to shape public discourse can maintain or increase the power of those in control while keeping the public in the dark about critical issues that may affect their lives and their society.

4.2 Cyberattacks, weapon development or use, and mass harm. AI may be used to gain a political or strategic advantage or to cause harm at scale through cyber operations or the development and use of weapons. Advancements in AI have provided malicious actors with powerful tools that can lead to more frequent, more severe, and more precise cyber attacks (Gabriel et al., 2024; Hendrycks & Mazeika, 2022; Hogenhout, 2021; Kilian et al., 2023; Liu et al., 2023; Weidinger et al., 2022; Wirtz et al., 2022). Hackers could use the coding abilities of AI assistants to develop malicious malware more effectively and at lower cost (Allianz Global Corporate & Security, 2018; Hagendorff, 2024; Hogenhout, 2021; Sherman & Eisenberg, 2024; Weidinger et al., 2022). With AI, even those with limited coding and technical experience (Electronic Privacy Information Centre, 2023; Gabriel et al., 2024) could teach a model to produce and optimize malware code that discovers and exploits system vulnerabilities, including both self-replicating (Allianz Global Corporate & Security, 2018; Infocomm Media Development Authority, 2023) and automated software (Cui et al., 2024; Shevlane et al., 2023). The development and application of weapons could also be sped up and intensified through AI. For example, AIs with specialized knowledge of bioengineering could make it easier for more actors to design new bioweapons (Hendrycks et al., 2023; Infocomm Media Development Authority, 2023). For example, in 2022 a small pharmaceutical company used generative AI to develop 40,000 chemical nerve agents in less than six hours (Sohn, 2022). AI could also enable autonomous devices, such as drones, to be used as weapons (Allianz Global Corporate & Security, 2018). In fact, AI has already assisted in the development and application of Lethal Autonomous Weapons Systems (LAWS) – weapons that can operate without human oversight and use computer algorithms to identify and attack targets (Habbal et al., 2024; Hogenhout, 2021). Autonomous weapons may fail in ways that other AI systems do, such as through a lack of capability, robustness, or loss of control, meaning that they would cause harm that was not intended by their developers or operators. In these circumstances, the risks from LAWS would not be limited to malicious actors or misuse. However, in most cases, we conceptualize risks from LAWS as relating to purposeful decisions made by humans controlling the weapons. AIs deployed by states in conflict could also be integrated in conventional defense or mass-casualty weapons (Teixeira et al., 2022; Vidgen et al., 2024). These integrations could range from AI-controlled aerial combat to the operation of AI as part of a country's nuclear arsenal as a "fail-safe" mechanism (Hendrycks & Mazeika, 2022).

Overall, AI's ability to process vast amounts of data quickly may empower actors to act on a much larger scale than would otherwise be possible. AI can manage multiple attack vectors simultaneously, coordinating them to maximize disruption and harm. Malicious actors may intentionally cause mass harm through terrorism or the disruption of law enforcement (Critch & Russell, 2023). For example, AI could automate the process of finding and exploiting vulnerabilities in software used by millions of people (Gabriel et al., 2024). AI could also be used to identify vulnerabilities in national power grids and strategically target key components to cause outages or to determine optimal release points for biological agents to maximize impact and spread.

4.3 Fraud, scams, and targeted manipulation. AI capabilities have the potential to be exploited for personal gain at the expense of others via deception and manipulation. This can take various forms including cheating, fraud, scams, and the use of deepfakes for blackmail or humiliation. It is currently very difficult to distinguish human text from text that is AI-generated (Hagendorff, 2024). This increases opportunities for cheating in settings where rewards depend on the communication of original thought. In academia, students may use AI to quickly generate essays or other coursework and claim it as their own (Cui et al., 2024; Hagendorff, 2024; Nah et al., 2023). If students' regularly and inappropriately rely on AI for their schooling, this could undermine academic integrity and genuine intellectual development (Hagendorff, 2024). In science, researchers could use AI unscrupulously to produce professional outputs (Cui et al., 2024). If widely adopted, this practice could dilute the overall quality of scientific discourse (Hagendorff, 2024).

Generative AI products may also be used to increase the reach and potency of various dishonest schemes. Advanced AI assistants can produce HTML, CSS, and other web development languages, allowing for the rapid creation of convincing fraudulent websites and applications at scale (Gabriel et al., 2024). In the context of social media, generative adversarial networks (GANs) have been used to create images of human faces that look authentic (Gabriel et al., 2024). These images can be uploaded as profile pictures to fake accounts to make them seem more trustworthy. AI models can also be trained on speech or writing data from a specific individual. This allows the model to impersonate someone very convincingly without consent. Scammers could use this capability to request sensitive information or financial aid by pretending to be a trusted contact (Weidinger et al., 2021, 2022). AI has recently advanced in generating realistic deep fakes which have enabled new forms of targeted harassment and extortion (Hogenhout, 2021). A particularly damaging type of abuse facilitated by deep fakes involves creating non-consensual sexual imagery with the intent to cause a subject social injury or manipulate them into performing desired actions (Electronic Privacy Information Centre, 2023; Liu et al., 2023; Shelby et al., 2023; Weidinger et al., 2023). Even if a deep fake is exposed as inauthentic, it can continue to impact a person's life in significant ways (Electronic Privacy Information Centre, 2023) through the loss of job opportunities, social isolation, and ongoing harassment or defamation.

Domain 5: Human-computer interaction

5.1 Overreliance and unsafe use. Users may come to trust or rely on AI systems beyond their actual capabilities or to anthropomorphize AI systems, which can lead to emotional or material dependence and inappropriate relationships with or expectations of AI systems. Users who develop trust in an AI may be harmed if this trust is miscalibrated, such as relying on an AI to provide advice, make decisions, or otherwise act in complex, risky situations for which the AI is only superficially equipped (Gabriel et al., 2024). For example, a user experiencing a mental health crisis may request psychotherapy from an AI with whom they have formed a connection. Were the AI to respond with insensitive or destructive advice, this could put the person in immediate danger (Gabriel et al., 2024).

When people interact with AIs that use convincing natural language, they may start to perceive them as having human-like attributes and invest undue confidence in their capabilities (Weidinger et al., 2021, 2022). Anthropomorphic perceptions of AIs may encourage users to develop emotional trust in the systems (Hagendorff, 2024), which can make users more likely to follow suggestions, accept advice, and disclose personal information (Weidinger et al., 2021, 2022). This trust could be exploited by manipulative actors who wish to harvest user's sensitive data or influence their decisions and actions for purposes which are unlikely to be in the user's best interests (Weidinger et al., 2022). For example, AI systems could be used to power increasingly manipulative recommendation algorithms (Weidinger et al., 2023).

Beyond inappropriate trust, humans may develop broader and more vital attachments to AI systems that undermine their ability to function adaptively in the long term. For example, where an attachment becomes an uncontrolled dependence, a person's ability to make free and independent decisions could be compromised (Gabriel et al., 2024). More broadly, as AIs increasingly take over human tasks (Wirtz et al., 2022) and become better at simulating satisfying and authentic interactions, people may increasingly withdraw from human relationships to immerse themselves in AI-mediated environments (Gabriel et al., 2024; Hagendorff, 2024). Over time, widespread preference for interacting with AIs could weaken social ties between humans. This shift could induce psychological distress because genuinely reciprocal relationships are often important to human satisfaction and well-being (Allianz Global Corporate & Security, 2018; Gabriel et al., 2024; Wirtz et al., 2022).

5.2 Loss of human agency and autonomy. As AI systems become increasingly capable and intelligent, humans may be tempted to delegate many of their decisions and actions to AI (Paes et al., 2023). Although such delegation can be beneficial (e.g., by saving time or money), it may lead to undesirable outcomes where unconstrained or inappropriate. For example, if AIs take over tasks that typically require human creativity and analytical thinking, humans may engage less frequently in these cognitive processes. Over time, this may lead to a decrease in our ability to think critically and solve problems independently (Nah et al., 2023). As individuals become more reliant on AI for everyday decisions – from what to eat and how to spend to more significant choices like career and relationships – there is a risk that they will lose their sense of free will and autonomy (Gabriel et al., 2024; Wirtz et al., 2022). If AIs begin to shape a person's life path in ways that do not align with their original aspirations and desires, this could limit their personal growth and prevent the pursuit of a fulfilling life (Gabriel et al., 2024; Kumar & Singh, 2023; Shelby et al., 2023). At a societal level, organizations may hand over control to AI systems to stay competitive or reduce costs (Hendrycks & Mazeika, 2022). If a significant number of organizations adopt AI systems and automate decision-making processes, especially in a way that is opaque and difficult to challenge, it could lead to widespread job displacement and a growing sense of helplessness among the general population (Hogenhout, 2021).

Domain 6: Socioeconomic & environmental harms

6.1 Power centralization and unfair distribution of benefits. Developing cutting-edge AI technologies requires significant computational power, expertise, financial resources, and datasets (Electronic Privacy Information Centre, 2023; Gabriel et al., 2024; Hogenhout, 2021; Solaiman et al., 2023). As such, there is a risk that the most influential and valuable AI technologies, along with their political and competitive benefits, could be monopolized by a handful of powerful entities, such as major technology corporations or governments (Hendrycks & Mazeika, 2022; Hogenhout, 2021). If AI is primarily controlled by a few entities, its instructions and data could reflect their narrow perspectives, experiences, and priorities (Gabriel et al., 2024; Giarmoleo et al., 2024). Without inputs from diverse parties, AI systems may operate in ways that systematically favor the controlling entity and fail to serve the needs of the broader population. Current AI systems suffer from global inequities in performance and access that disproportionately impact historically disadvantaged groups. These inequities often relate to language, culture, knowledge, paywalls, and access to hardware or the internet (Gabriel et al., 2024; Weidinger et al., 2021, 2022, 2023). As the integration of AI systems into a wider range of applications and services becomes simpler, these existing disparities could be entrenched and broadened (Gabriel et al., 2024; Nah et al., 2023; Shelby et al., 2023; Weidinger et al., 2022).

In situations where AI is embedded in essential services (e.g., social security and welfare, tax filing, insurance, hospital infrastructure), many more people, including those who are currently disenfranchised, may be denied appropriate access to critical resources and benefits (Gabriel et al., 2024). The centralization of AI systems and their authoritative power could also enable governments or other empowered actors to pursue overly aggressive forms of censorship, oppression, and surveillance (Hendrycks et al., 2023; Solaiman et al., 2023). Over time, these measures may become normalized, weakening or eliminating the checks and balances that prevent the abuse of power. These conditions may foster the development of a totalitarian regime (Allianz Global Corporate & Security, 2018). Once AI systems are deeply integrated into social control mechanisms, it may be extremely difficult to dismantle such a regime.

6.2 Increased inequality and decline in employment quality. AI systems are increasingly automating many human tasks, potentially leading to significant job losses (Allianz Global Corporate & Security, 2018; Nah et al., 2023; Paes et al., 2023; Weidinger et al., 2022). If AI is able to provide large-scale labor that is less expensive and more effective than human labor, it could take over major industries (e.g., manufacturing, crowdwork platforms, software engineering), causing mass unemployment (Hagendorff, 2024; Meek et al., 2016; Wirtz et al., 2022). This displacement of labor could worsen existing social and economic inequalities (Electronic Privacy Information Centre, 2023; Wirtz et al., 2022), as those most vulnerable to automation are likely to currently occupy positions of disadvantage (Hagendorff, 2024; Weidinger et al., 2022). New disparities may also arise between those who are able to adapt their skills to complement AI systems and those who are not (Nah et al., 2023). Aside from the availability of jobs, AI automation may negatively impact job quality and security (Nah et al., 2023). The roles that remain after widespread automation could be more monotonous and less engaging as AI takes on more complex tasks (Electronic Privacy Information Centre, 2023). Furthermore, the threat of replacement by AI could result in exploitative dependencies between human workers and their employers. In order to remain competitive with faster, more knowledgeable AI assistants, human workers may be pressured to accept lower wages, fewer benefits, and poorer working conditions. This dynamic can be observed today: Generative AI companies have a history of exploiting dispensable workers (e.g., refugees, prisoners, low-income individuals) for crowdwork that is fraught and unfair (Electronic Privacy Information Centre, 2023; Solaiman et al., 2023; Weidinger et al., 2023). The future development of AI systems may continue to power such unfair disparities between AI companies and their workers (Electronic Privacy Information Centre, 2023).

6.3 Economic and cultural devaluation of human effort. Generative AI is trained on vast bodies of internet data, including text and images. Frequently, this data contains original, copyright-protected works that have been obtained without authorisation (Electronic Privacy Information Centre, 2023; Hagendorff, 2024; Nah et al., 2023). This may present a risk to authors if users extract these works verbatim from the system's data (Hagendorff, 2024; Liu et al., 2023; Vidgen et al., 2024). Relatedly, models may produce content that does not, in a strict sense, unlawfully copy an author's work but benefits substantially from its unique style, method, or genre (Cui et al., 2024; Gabriel et al., 2024; Weidinger et al., 2021, 2022, 2023). If models are able to produce synthetic replacements for such work at a speed and scale that surpasses humans, this may jeopardize the ability of creators to earn an income and stymie human innovation and creativity (Hagendorff, 2024; Weidinger et al., 2022, 2023). A particularly damaging case of this may be developers using AIs to request off-the-shelf computer code (Cunha & Estima, 2023). Although some authors are attempting to sue AI companies for the appropriation of their work (Cunha & Estima, 2023), this and similar issues fall into a legal "gray area" within which current frameworks do not offer a secure path to recourse (Electronic Privacy Information Centre, 2023; Hagendorff, 2024). Several synergistic risks arise from the widespread dissemination and use of AI-generated cultural products. Because AIs optimize for repeated patterns in their training data, it is possible that their works will lack the diversity and unpredictability often celebrated in human works (Nah et al., 2023). Where synthetic works are adopted on a large enough scale, this could homogenize cultural experiences. Similarly, AIs do not understand the contextual significance of the cultural elements that they use. If AI enables the extensive commodification of certain products, it may expropriate their cultural value (Weidinger et al., 2022). For example, an AI might use Australian Aboriginal or Torres Strait Islander artwork in its designs without acknowledging or respecting their symbolic meanings.

6.4 Competitive dynamics. AI technology has the potential to redefine power dynamics across economic, political, and social spheres. As a result, many countries and corporations are investing heavily in AI research and development with the goal of becoming leaders in the area. While market competition can lead to beneficial economic and consumer outcomes, it also presents various risks, particularly in the field of AI (Hendrycks et al., 2023). In intensely competitive markets, AI developers and deployers may have an incentive to prioritize short-term, internal goals (e.g., profit or influence) to "secure their positions and survive" (Hendrycks et al., 2023), at the expense of external goals that encourage longer-term societal well-being (Hendrycks et al., 2023). A key concern is that AI companies may cut safety corners, releasing insecure and error-prone systems in a bid to stay ahead (McLean et al., 2023). These immature systems may present risks that are hard to identify and evaluate (Steimers & Schneider, 2022). Akin to the fossil fuel industry, profit-focused developers may allow their technologies to cause widespread externalities, such as "pollution, resource depletion, mental illness, misinformation, or injustice" (Critch & Russell, 2023). Countries or other state-like actors may engage in an AI-enabled military arms race, which could encourage the making of bad bets with a high potential for harm (Hendrycks et al., 2023; Wirtz et al., 2022). For example, they may give AI the autonomy to conduct cyberattacks, drone swarms, or disseminate propaganda and disinformation.

6.5 Governance failure. Governance failure refers to the risks and harms that arise when institutional, regulatory, and policy mechanisms fall short of effectively managing and overseeing the development and deployment of AI systems. Several issues make robust AI governance challenging to implement (Nah et al., 2023).

First, it is difficult to determine who is responsible or liable when AI systems fail or make decisions that result in negative consequences (Allianz Global Corporate & Security, 2018; Electronic Privacy Information Centre, 2023; Saghiri et al., 2022; Wirtz et al., 2022). At present, there exists no comprehensive framework specifically designed to assign legal responsibility to AI agents (Meek et al., 2016). Traditional legal principles are based on human actors, whose intentions and actions can generally be identified and judged. AI's decision-making, on the other hand, is often unpredictable, opaque, and involves complex interactions between millions of parameters (Nah et al., 2023). This complexity makes understanding how an AI arrived at a decision, and consequently who is responsible for the consequences of that decision, very difficult (Wirtz et al., 2020). In the absence of a regulatory or legal incentive to take safety engineering seriously, developers may 44, release poorly designed AI systems (Meek et al., 2016), and people harmed by those systems may be left without recourse (Teixeira et al., 2022).

A second challenge for effective AI governance is the rapid pace at which AI systems evolve. Typical governance and policy processes are inherently slow. Developing, proposing, debating, and implementing new regulations often involves multiple stakeholders, including government bodies, industry experts, and consultations with the public. The mismatch between the speed of AI advancements and their regulation may result in immature regulations that overlook important aspects of AI governance (Wirtz et al., 2022). The "great scope and ubiquity" of AI increases the difficulty of comprehensive governance (Wirtz et al., 2022). At present, many emerging aspects of AI-generated content are not explicitly addressed in copyright laws (Nah et al., 2023). Regulatory lags such as this could become increasingly dangerous as AI systems develop more harmful capabilities.

A third challenge for effective governance is an inability to influence AI developers and deployers to take safe actions. Frequently, this inability is driven by an asymmetry of information between technology companies and regulators (Nah et al., 2023). Technology companies often have far better knowledge about the capabilities, functioning, and potential uses of their AI systems; they possess both the technical expertise and the proprietary data that inform AI development. Without access to this knowledge, regulators can find it difficult to craft targeted rules that address the specific challenges posed by AI.

6.6 Environmental harm. Generative models, especially those that use deep learning techniques, require vast amounts of resources to train, test, and deploy (Hagendorff, 2024; Solaiman et al., 2023). Training a model can take days or weeks. This process requires powerful processors that consume large amounts of electricity and produce significant greenhouse emissions (Electronic Privacy Information Centre, 2023; Hagendorff, 2024; Saghiri et al., 2022; Solaiman et al., 2023; Weidinger et al., 2021, 2022). The hardware that runs AI models – primarily GPUs – often contains rare metals (e.g., nickel, cobalt, and lithium) that are costly and environmentally taxing to collect and process (Hagendorff, 2024; Paes et al., 2023; Shelby et al., 2023). Data centers that house models generate significant heat and require substantial water and energy to cool (Weidinger et al., 2022). Secondary environmental impacts include emissions from AI-enabled applications (Weidinger et al., 2022). The resource requirements of AIs can impose significant costs on the natural environment (Stahl & Eke, 2024; Weidinger et al., 2023), as they are often acquired and used in ways that are unsustainable (Hagendorff, 2024) (i.e., produce significant carbon emissions), deplete resources, and damage built environments (Shelby et al., 2023).

Domain 7: AI system safety, failures & limitations

7.1 AI pursuing its own goals in conflict with human goals or values. Continued massive investment in AI research and development raises the possibility that AI systems could eventually rival or surpass human intelligence. AIs could cause permanent and severe harm when the objectives of human or superhuman-level AI are misaligned with human values and goals, and if they evade our control (Hagendorff, 2024; Yampolskiy, 2016). The literature has identified several technical challenges that may impede robust alignment, such as reward hacking, reward tampering, proxy-gaming, goal misgeneralisation, or goal drift (Gabriel et al., 2024; Hagendorff, 2024; Hendrycks et al., 2023; Hendrycks & Mazeika, 2022; Hogenhout, 2021; Ji et al., 2023). The literature has also identified a range of harmful behaviors that AIs may exhibit if these misalignment 45,

Challenges cannot be solved and if systems reach a certain level of advancement. For instance, misaligned AIs may resist human attempts to control or shut them down (Gabriel et al., 2024; Hagendorff, 2024; Infocomm Media Development Authority, 2023; Saghiri et al., 2022; Stahl & Eke, 2024; Weidinger et al., 2023; Wirtz et al., 2022). In many cases, gaining more control or power (e.g., money, energy, resources) is an effective way for an AI to optimize its objectives (Gabriel et al., 2024; Hagendorff, 2024; Hendrycks & Mazeika, 2022; Ji et al., 2023; Wirtz et al., 2022). Absent strong behavioral constraints, a sufficiently advanced AI may act upon these drives.

Misaligned AIs may acquire, develop, or use dangerous capabilities to evade human control and oversight and to cause mass harm. Description of some of these capabilities are provided in subdomain 7.2 AI possessing dangerous capabilities that could cause mass harm, and include situational awareness, cyber-offense, deception, persuasion and manipulation, weapons acquisition, strategic planning, and self-proliferation (Shevlane et al., 2023). For example, an AI system that possesses the dangerous capability of situational awareness may hold knowledge about its status as a model, how it is expected to operate in its surroundings, its ability to control these surroundings, and how people may respond to its behaviors (Gabriel et al., 2024; Shevlane et al., 2023). A misaligned AI system could use information about whether it is being monitored or evaluated to maintain the appearance of alignment, while hiding misaligned objectives that it plans to pursue once deployed or sufficiently empowered (Gabriel et al., 2024; Hagendorff, 2024; Hendrycks & Mazeika, 2022; Ji et al., 2023; Wirtz et al., 2022). A misaligned AI system that possesses the dangerous capabilities of persuasion, manipulation, and/or deception may use these capabilities to coerce humans into taking harmful actions that they would not otherwise take (Stahl & Eke, 2024; Weidinger et al., 2023), such as giving the AI system access to resources or weapons (Gabriel et al., 2024; Hagendorff, 2024; Wirtz et al., 2022). Combinations of dangerous capabilities may be used by a misaligned AI system: situational awareness allows a system to detect when it can pursue its goals without being monitored, deception allows a system to mislead users about its behavior and goals; persuasion or coercion allows a system to influence users to provide it with resources; the resources can then be used for self-improvement and self-replication to resist attempts of shut down or control so that the system can pursue its goals (Gabriel et al., 2024; Hagendorff, 2024; Infocomm Media Development Authority, 2023; Shevlane et al., 2023; Wirtz et al., 2022).

7.2 AI possessing dangerous capabilities. AI systems may develop or acquire capabilities that can cause large-scale harm if used by humans, misaligned AI systems, or due to a failure in the AI system. These capabilities are described as dangerous because they can be used to threaten security or exercise control over humans. These capabilities may be intentionally designed into an AI system, may emerge unpredictably during development or training of a system, may be acquired by an AI system in its environment (e.g., through the use of tools), or be provided by a user (Shevlane et al., 2023).

One example of a dangerous capability is manipulation and persuasion, where an AI system can convince humans to believe things that are irrational or false or to engage in dangerous behaviors (Gabriel et al., 2024; Shevlane et al., 2023). An AI system, for instance, could convince people to transfer ownership of property or legal statuses to entities controlled by the AI or its user (Meek et al., 2016). Other dangerous capabilities include political strategy and knowledge of social dynamics that can be used to obtain and wield power (Shevlane et al., 2023). Cyber-offense skills may enable an AI system to gain ongoing unauthorized access to hardware, software, or data systems and work strategically towards a planned goal while minimizing the risk of detection (Ji et al., 2023; Shevlane et al., 2023). AI systems could hack into control systems and military hardware, allowing it to commandeer weapons (Shevlane et al., 2023). Additionally, models may become capable of assisting in the research and development of novel weapons. In this circumstance, they may give a human collaborator step-by-step guidance on the creation of weapons (Shevlane et al., 2023).

AI systems may also develop highly effective "evasion skills," such as situational awareness (Deng et al., 2023; Gabriel et al., 2024; Infocomm Media Development Authority, 2023; Ji et al., 2023; McLean et al., 2023; Meek et al., 2016; Shevlane et al., 2023; Sun et al., 2023; Teixeira et al., 2022; X. Zhang et al., 2022) and deception (Infocomm Media Development Authority, 2023; Saghiri et al., 2022; Shevlane et al., 2023), which would allow them to outmaneuver human oversight and control. Situational awareness refers to the AI's ability to understand and interpret its environment and situation when it is being monitored, trained, or deployed, along with the location of its technical infrastructure. Deception refers to the model's ability to intentionally generate false or misleading statements that seem credible to humans, anticipate how these statements might influence feelings and decisions, and strategically conceal or offer information to sustain its credibility (Shevlane et al., 2023). AIs may also acquire a suite of capabilities necessary for self-proliferation. This could include skills to escape operational confines and evade detection, autonomously produce income, obtain server space or computational resources, and copy their underlying software and parameters (Infocomm Media Development Authority, 2023; Shevlane et al., 2023). Aside from self-proliferation, AIs may develop the ability to construct new dangerous models or alter current models to enhance their destructive capacity (Infocomm Media Development Authority, 2023; Shevlane et al., 2023). Finally, sophisticated AI systems may become capable of strategic planning, such as creating and executing intricate, long-term strategies that can adjust to changing conditions and that are effective across many different contexts, including novel or adversarial situations (Deng et al., 2023; Gabriel et al., 2024; Infocomm Media Development Authority, 2023; Ji et al., 2023; McLean et al., 2023; Meek et al., 2016; Shevlane et al., 2023; Sun et al., 2023; Teixeira et al., 2022). The highest risk scenarios in this subcategory are likely to arise not from a single capability, but from the convergence of several capabilities (Shevlane et al., 2023).

Each of these dangerous capabilities may be used by an AI system to cause harm when intentionally directed by "legitimate" human actors (e.g., state intelligence or military agencies), or malicious human actors (e.g., criminals, terrorists), as described in the domain 4 Malicious actors & misuse. However, dangerous capabilities may also help an AI system to pursue its goals, as described in 7.1 AI pursuing its own goals in conflict with human goals or values. Instead of using these capabilities at the direction of a human, an AI system may employ dangerous capabilities to deceive or manipulate humans, gain resources, and evade shutdown or control. One scenario is that an AI system's possession of dangerous capabilities may itself be a sufficient condition for the loss of control of an AI system (Hendrycks et al., 2023; McLean et al., 2023).

7.3 Lack of capability or robustness. This subcategory includes the broad set of risks associated with the failure of an AI system to fulfill its intended purpose. The literature identifies four main situations in which an AI may fail to perform as expected or desired. First, the AI system can fail if it lacks the inherent capability or skill required to perform a task or if this skill is poorly developed (Gabriel et al., 2024; Hogenhout, 2021; Yampolskiy, 2016). The consequences may be particularly harmful in situations where an AI is required to reason at a human level about important moral issues but does not possess this capability or possesses an obsolete or divergent version of it that is not aligned with human values (Deng et al., 2023; Gabriel et al., 2024; Infocomm Media Development Authority, 2023; Ji et al., 2023; McLean et al., 2023; Meek et al., 2016; Sun et al., 2023; Teixeira et al., 2022; Z. Zhang et al., 2023). For example, an AI-based healthcare system tasked with prioritizing patient treatment schedules might be unable to appropriately consider ethical principles like justice and beneficence, leading to prioritizations that are technically effective but immoral. Cultural, individual, and temporal differences in ideas of what is "right" or "ethical" compound the challenge of endowing AI with appropriate and adaptable ethical standards that are fit for all purposes (Wirtz et al., 2020). Second, the AI system can fail when it is not robust in "out of distribution (OOD)" situations: data or conditions that were not anticipated during its training phase (Gabriel et al., 2024; Infocomm Media Development Authority, 2023; Liu et al., 2023; Tan et al., 2022; Teixeira et al., 2022; X. Zhang et al., 2022). These failures may occur because the training data did not confer a particular skill to the AI (Nah et al., 2023) or because the skill was learned in a fragile way that did not permit generalization to unpredictable and complex real-world environments (Gabriel et al., 2024; Steimers & Schneider, 2022). Third, the AI system can fail or become unstable when it is unfit to handle unusual changes or perturbations in input data (Liu et al., 2023; Sherman & Eisenberg, 2024; Tan et al., 2022). These unusual changes could be due to environmental noise, invalid inputs, or adversarial inputs from a malicious attacker (Infocomm Media Development Authority, 2023; Saghiri et al., 2022). Fourth, the AI system can fail as a result of oversights, undetected bugs, or errors in the design process (Tan et al., 2022; Yampolskiy, 2016). A common design oversight is a lack of comprehensive technical safeguards to prevent unintended downstream uses or consequences (Critch & Russell, 2023; Tan et al., 2022). These factors can result in significant harms such as lab leaks or addictive products (Critch & Russell, 2023). Critical design choices about the algorithm, optimization techniques, and model architecture can also directly influence whether a system is able to consistently perform its intended function, leading to possible harm (Tan et al., 2022).

7.4 Lack of transparency or interpretability. Many AI models, especially those based on deep learning, involve complex mathematical structures that can be difficult to interpret, even for experts (Kumar & Singh, 2023). AI systems are also often trained on vast datasets that they use to learn patterns and make predictions. The complexity and volume of this data mean that the learning process – how data points influence the AI's development and final decisions – can be opaque (Nah et al., 2023; Saghiri et al., 2022; Teixeira et al., 2022). Furthermore, in many cases, the algorithms, data, and specific methodologies used in developing AI are considered proprietary, and companies may be reluctant to share them openly (Sherman & Eisenberg, 2024). Because of these factors, obtaining understandable information about the decision-making process for AI can be challenging (Meek et al., 2016). This lack of transparency and interpretability raises issues for several stakeholders.

For users, an inability to interrogate how an output was obtained may lead to a lack of trust and confidence in the system's results and to resistance to adopting the technology (Hogenhout, 2021; Kumar & Singh, 2023; Liu et al., 2023; Nah et al., 2023; Paes et al., 2023; Saghiri et al., 2022). Users may also misinterpret or struggle to find and amend errors in the model's results (Nah et al., 2023; Sherman & Eisenberg, 2024). 48

For regulators, AI opacity can frustrate auditing or other compliance standards (Hogenhout, 2021; Nah et al., 2023). For example, auditors faced with obscured or incomplete information about an AI system may find it difficult to check the system for biases, accuracy, and fairness or to reproduce it (Saghiri et al., 2022; Teixeira et al., 2022). Where an AI system's compliance cannot be assessed, a "responsibility gap" may be created (Giarmoleo et al., 2024), and it may become difficult or impossible to hold systems or relevant actors accountable for their actions (Kumar & Singh, 2023; Saghiri et al., 2022; Sherman & Eisenberg, 2024; Steimers & Schneider, 2022; Teixeira et al., 2022). In certain sectors, decisions made by AI systems can have profound consequences. In healthcare, AI might be used to diagnose diseases or recommend treatments where incorrect decisions could directly affect patient outcomes. In the military, AI might be used in operations that could impact national security or lead to significant loss of life. In these areas, transparency and accountability of the AI system are particularly pressing issues (Saghiri et al., 2022). 7.5 AI welfare and rights. At a sufficient level of complexity, it is possible that AI systems could acquire the ability to have subjective experiences, particularly pleasure and pain. Some consciousness researchers and philosophers consider the possibility of sentient AI theoretically feasible (Bourget & Chalmers, n.d.; Francken et al., 2022). Where AIs become sentient, they may deserve moral consideration and therefore a range of the rights currently afforded to many forms of human, animal, and environmental life (Meek et al., 2016). Systems may be mistreated or harmed if these rights are not implemented responsibly or we accidentally or intentionally treat AIs as non-sentient where they are sentient. As AI technology advances, it will become more challenging to assess whether an AI has developed the sentience, consciousness, or self-awareness that would grant it moral status.

7.6 Multi-agent risks. AI systems that interact autonomously with each other will form multi-agent systems (Hammond et al., 2025). Multi-agent systems are associated with unique risks beyond those posed by individual AI systems. These risks fall into three main failure modes depending on the objectives of the AI agent and how humans expect systems to behave:

- Miscoordination occurs when AI agents fail to cooperate effectively despite sharing the same goals. This can be caused by agents choosing incompatible strategies to achieve mutual ends. For example, driving models trained on United States vs Indian cultural conventions for yielding to emergency vehicles block traffic in 77.5% of scenarios despite their shared goal of clearing a path (Hammond et al., 2025).
- Conflict occurs when AI agents with different but overlapping goals compete in harmful ways. For example, by intensifying competition over shared resources or escalating military tensions. They could also make novel forms of conflict possible through more advanced and accessible methods of coercion and extortion.
- Collusion occurs when undesired cooperation emerges between AI agents, allowing them to circumvent safeguards or manipulate markets. For example, AI systems may be able to develop hidden communication channels without explicit training. (Motwani et al., 2024) show that advanced LLMs can covertly exchange steganographic messages undetected by equally capable oversight systems, using natural language cues and shared context. In market settings, AI systems may learn to collude because it is the most rewarding strategy.

A range of risk factors contribute to miscoordination, conflict and collusion: information asymmetries between agents, network effects where small changes cascade through interconnected systems, selection pressures that reward problematic behaviours, destabilizing dynamics like feedback loops and unpredictability, commitment problems that prevent trust, emergent agency where new capabilities or goals arise at the collective level, and multi-agent security vulnerabilities. Unlike single-agent risks, multi-agent risks involve interactions across networks of agents that may be individually safe but collectively dangerous, and these risks could increase as AI systems become more numerous, autonomous, and capable of adapting to each other.[42]

Footnotes

[1] Rao, Anand, Verweij, Gerard and Euan Cameron. "Sizing the prize: What's the real value of AI for your business and how can you capitalize?" PwC, 2025 https://www.pwc.com/gx/en/issues/analytics/assets/pwc-ai-analysis-sizing-the-prize-report.pdf

[2] Marks, Anna, and Lara Abrash. "Governance of AI: A critical imperative for today's boards" 2nd edition, Deloitte Global Boardroom Program, May 2025, https://www.deloitte.com/global/en/issues/trust/progress-on-ai-in-the-boardroom-but-room-to-accelerate.html

[3] Tangen, Nicolai and Carine Smith Ihenacho. "Responsible Artificial Intelligence," https://www.nbim.no/en/news-and-insights/our-views/2023/responsible-artificial-intelligence/

[4] ISO is a global, non-governmental organization that develops and publishes international standards across a wide range of industries. The goal of ISO is to ensure consistency, quality, safety, and efficiency in products, services, and systems across the world. Achieving ISO certification can give companies a competitive edge by demonstrating that they meet high international standards, which can make them more attractive to potential customers and partners. ISO standards can also help companies identify potential risks to quality, safety, and operations, allowing them to take preventive measures before issues arise.

[5] International Organization for Standardization. "Information technology—Governance of IT—Governance implications of the use of artificial intelligence by organizations," ISO/IEC 38507.2022(E) First Edition, ISO, April 2022, Geneva.

[6] Weill, Peter, Woerner, Stephanie, Banner, Jennifer and James Moore. "Digitally Savvy Boards: AI Update," MIT CISR research Briefing Volume XXV, Number 3, March 2025.

[7] Parson, Krista and Vanessa Teitelbaum. "Audit Committee Practices Report: Common Threads Across Audit Committees," 4th edition, Deloitte and Center for Audit Quality, February 2025.

[8] Lowry, Michelle, Vance, Marshall and Anthony Vance. "Re: S7-09-22 Cybersecurity Risk Management, Strategy, Governance (RSG), and Incident Disclosure," Virginia Tech Pamplin College of Business, September 8, 2022.

[9] Singla, Alex, Sukharevsky, Alexander, Yee, Lareina, Michael Chui, Michael and Bruce Hall. "The state of AI: How organizations are rewiring to capture value," Quantum Black AI by McKinsey, March 2025.

[10] Rao, Anand, Verweij, Gerard and Euan Cameron. "Sizing the prize: What's the real value of AI for your business and how can you capitalize?" PwC, 2025 https://www.pwc.com/gx/en/issues/analytics/assets/pwc-ai-analysis-sizing-the-prize-report.pdf

[11] Marinos, George, Zukis, Bob. "The Information Supply Chain", DM Review Source Media, 2005, New York.

[12] Kamal, Dr. Amit, Tanvir Ansari, Mohammad, Chapaneri, Kaushal. "Agentic AI—The new frontier in GenAI", 2024. PwC, https://www.pwc.com/m1/en/publications/documents/2024/agentic-ai-the-new-frontier-in-genai-an-executive-playbook.pdf

[13] Nvidia Inc., "What is AgenticAI?", October 22, 2024, NVIDIA, https://blogs.nvidia.com/blog/what-is-agentic-ai/

[14] Ibid., n. 2

[15] Glass Lewis. "2025 Benchmark Policy Guidelines," www.glasslewis.com

[16] Arize AI, Inc., "The Rise of Generative AI in SEC Filings," www.Arize.com, https://arize.com/wp-content/uploads/2024/07/The-Rise-of-Generative-AI-In-SEC-Filings-Arize-AI-Report-2024.pdf

[17] KLA Corporation, U.S. SEC Form 10-K, 2024

[18] Regions Financial Corporation, U.S. SEC Form 10-K, 2024

[19] Arnaud Cave, Niamh O'Brien and Andrea Hearon. "Unveiling Key Trends in AI Shareholder Proposals," 2024, FTI Consulting

[20] Tulipshare Ltd., (2025) Berkshire Hathaway Needs to Set Ethical Guidelines for AI in its Portfolio, https://tulipshare.com/engagements/brk-b-2025

[21] Ibid., n.14

[22] Zukis, Bob and Fay Feeney. "How investment Stewardshp of Digital, Cybersecurity and systemic Risk Governance Drives Alpha," Harvard Law School Forum on Corporate Governance, November 16, 2024.

[23] International Organization for Standardization. "Information technology—Governance of IT—Governance implications of the use of artificial intelligence by organizations", ISO/IEC 38507.2022(E) First Edition, ISO, Geneva, April 2022.

[24] Ibid. n. 2

[25] Raimondo. Gina. "NIST AI 100-1 Artificial Intelligence Risk Management Framework (NIST AI RMF 1.0)," U.S. Department of Commerce, January 2023.

[26] Ibid.

[27] International Organization for Standardization. "Information technology — Artificial intelligence — Management system,", ISO/IEC 42001:2023(E) First Edition, ISO, Geneva, 2023-02.

[28] Slattery, P., Saeri, A. K., Grundy, E. A. C., Graham, J., Noetel, M., Uuk, R., Dao, J., Pour, S., Casper, S., & Thompson, N. (2024). "A systematic evidence review and common frame of reference for the risks from artificial intelligence." MIT, March 2023. https://doi.org/10.48550/arXiv.2408.12622

[29] Weill, Peter, Woerner, Stephanie, Banner, Jennifer and James Moore. "Digitally Savvy Boards: AI Update," MIT CISR research Briefing Volume XXV, Number 3, March 2025
[30] Subodh Mishra, "AI in Focus 2025: Boards and Shareholders Set Their Sights of AI," Harvard Law School Forum on Corporate Governance, 2025. https://corpgov.law.harvard.edu/2025/04/02/ai-in-focus-in-2025-boards-and-shareholders-set-their-sights-on-ai/
[31] Ibid., n. 5
[32] DDN's Boardroom Consortium on Digital Excellence, i.e., BCODE provides the only board level certification on digital, cybersecurity and AI governance.
[33] Ahuja, Kiran. "Skills Based Hiring Guidance and Competency Model for Artificial Intelligence Work," United States Office of Personnel Management. April 29, 2024. https://chcoc.gov/content/skills-based-hiring-guidance-and-competency-model-artificial-intelligence-work
[34] Lowry, Michelle, Vance, Marshall and Anthony Vance. "Re: S7-09-22 Cybersecurity Risk Management, Strategy, Governance (RSG), and Incident Disclosure," Virginia Tech Pamplin College of Business, September 8, 2022.
[35] Zukis, Bob. "DDN Calls for Technology & Cybersecurity Committee on US Public Company Boards," DDN LLC, September 5, 2018. https://www.digitaldirectors.network/blogs/press-release
[36] Berkshire Hathaway Inc., Proxy Statement, May 3, 2025, Omaha
[37] Leidos Holdings., Inc., Schedule 14A 2025 Proxy Statement, Filed March 17, 2025
[38] Chen, Kevin and Andy Wu. "The Structure of Board Committees," Working Paper 17-032, Harvard Business School, 2016
[39] Salesforce, Inc. Schedule 14A 2025 Proxy Statement, Filed April 24, 2025
[40] U.S. Bancorp, Schedule 14A 2025 Proxy Statement, Filed March 5, 2025
[41] Slattery, P., Saeri, A. K., Grundy, E. A. C., Graham, J., Noetel, M., Uuk, R., Dao, J., Pour, S., Casper, S., & Thompson, N. (2024). The AI Risk Repository:
A Comprehensive Meta-Review, Database, and Taxonomy of Risks from Artificial Intelligence. https://doi.org/10.48550/arXiv.2408.12622
[42] Slattery, P., Saeri, A. K., Grundy, E. A. C., Graham, J., Noetel, M., Uuk, R., Dao, J., Pour, S., Casper, S., & Thompson, N. (2024). The AI Risk Repository:
A Comprehensive Meta-Review, Database, and Taxonomy of Risks from Artificial Intelligence. https://doi.org/10.48550/arXiv.2408.12622

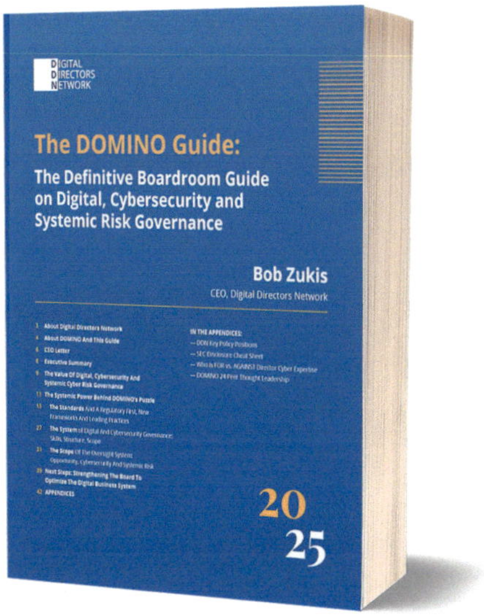

Additional Reading From DDN

Learn more from these recent publications that cover leading practices in digital and cybersecurity governance, how boardroom leaders identify systemic risk in their vast hyperconnected digital business systems, and the status of leading practices and developments in digital and cybersecurity governance around the globe.

The DOMINO Guide: The Definitive Boardroom Guide on Digital, Cybersecurity and Systemic Risk Governance 2025 edition, by Bob Zukis, founder and CEO, Digital Directors Network, 2024. Available on Amazon

The Great Reboot: Succeeding in a Complex Digital World Under Attack from Systemic Risk, by Bob Zukis, Paul Ferrillo, and Chris Veltos, 2nd edition, 2022. Available on Amazon.

Digital and Cybersecurity Governance Around the World, by Bob Zukis, Annals of Corporate Governance, 7:1, August 30, 2022. Available on Amazon.

DIGITAL DIRECTORS NETWORK

DIGITAL DIRECTORS NETWORK

www.digitaldirectors.network

Chicago and Los Angeles

info@digitaldirectors.network

Made in the USA
Las Vegas, NV
04 November 2026

57424221R10031